DRAMATICALLY
Zen

A GUIDEBOOK TO LIVING YOUR BEST LIFE

ANGELA URQUHART

 **FriesenPress**

Suite 300 - 990 Fort St
Victoria, BC, Canada, V8V 3K2
www.friesenpress.com

ISBN
978-1-77097-501-9 (Hardcover)
978-1-77097-502-6 (Paperback)
978-1-77097-503-3 (eBook)

1. Reference, Personal & Practical Guides

Distributed to the trade by The Ingram Book Company

TABLE OF CONTENTS

Dedicated to my Nonno.
This is my thank you.

PROLOGUE

Dramatically Zen: A theatric and expressive action or emotion in the effort to reach a peaceful state of being.
—Angela Urquhart, 2011

To me, being Dramatically Zen is an honest definition of how life works out. Sometimes things don't go as planned in our quest for personal enlightenment. We encounter roadblocks, confusion, and randomness. I accept and embrace this and, as a result, my life is always interesting. I'll never be an even-keeled person who isn't affected by emotions. I've always been, and always will be, a dramatic and fun-loving individual who seeks out the magnificence in the world, aspires for peace, and dreams as big as I possibly can.

The journey is the destination, and though I may never reach true "Zen" status, I'll live the best version of myself dramatically trying to get there.

When I made the bold decision to travel, something in my inner paradigm system shifted, filling me with new energy. This new magical energy was my ammunition for designing a life I was excited about living. The more I meditated and the more I looked inward, I recognized a fire within me—a burning desire for a life of magnitude just waiting to be unleashed.

It was the start of a new life.

My journey overseas provided me with the experiences I needed to heal, find strength, and live my dreams. My life went from having no direction or purpose to one filled with meaning and happiness.

Since returning home from my travels, I've adapted my transformational experiences to this book. Each chapter offers a different life lesson revealed to me during my time in Thailand, Australia, and Bali, all of which contributed to me becoming the best version of myself.

I'm not trying to reinvent the wheel as to how you should live and appreciate your life. Instead, I revisited some of the most simplistic life lessons that I, and many others, may have neglected to follow or have forgotten over the years. Each life lesson highlights the little things you can do to make your day-to-day just a little happier and put you on your own blissful journey. It doesn't take a trip around the world, but it does take a visit inside your soul.

Practice these life lessons to begin taking action to reach your goals, find your ultimate happiness, and become your best self.

Dramatically Zen. It's not just a book, it's a lifestyle.

INTRODUCTION

*"Our lives are not determined by what happens to us but by how
we react to what happens, not by what life brings to us, but by the
attitude we bring to life. A positive attitude causes a chain reaction
of positive thoughts, events, and outcomes. It is a catalyst, a spark
that creates extraordinary results."*
—Anon

To understand how I ended up traveling to Thailand, it's important to know how I grew up. Being half-Italian, half-Scottish
was an interesting mix, but the Italian influence dominated my life
experiences and decisions, including, later on, my decision to travel.

For 15 years growing up, every morning at 7:30 a.m., my mom
and dad went to work, and our Italian grandparents on my mom's
side, otherwise known as Nonno and Nonna, arrived at our house to
baby-sit my brother, Dave, and me.

The morning routine included a few specific practices: my Nonna
dressed me and styled my hair, which I insisted look like "Rainbow
Brite" (which called for hair half-up), while my Nonno prepared
the strongest coffee that was two points away from being molasses.
Then every day at noon, my Nonno would pick us up from school
and bring us to their house for lunch where we'd indulge in plates
of carb-filled goodness. After school, we'd return to my Nonno and
Nonna's house until our parents came home from work. And at least

twice a week, we would have family dinners at their house, consisting of more carb-filled goodness.

Dave and I adored our routine. The only break in the merriment
with our grandparents was when they took escape from the harsh
Canadian winters for six weeks and vacationed in Acapulco, Mexico.
While my brother and I cringed at being without them (which
also meant that after school we had to be babysat by a local group
of nuns), I was mesmerized by their enthusiasm at their impend-
ing travels.

Unable to contain his excitement, my Nonno lined up his
suitcases at the end of his driveway and sat in the garage hours in
advance to wait for the coach bus to pick them up and take them
to the airport. The garage, for Italians, serves as living room number
two, decked out with similar, if not nicer, furniture than indoors,
minus the plastic on the couches. It was the perfect spot for viewing
any event happening on the street, and the garage was the ideal
waiting room for their transit. Their anticipation and excitement of
the trip to Mexico was palpable.

After nearly two months of their absence, which seemed like an
eternity to me, I eagerly awaited my Nonno and Nonna's return
from the mysterious foreign location and relished in their stories.
Even at a young age, I felt a pang of tan envy when I observed their
beautifully bronzed skin. Little did I know it at the time, but my
curiosity about my Nonno and Nonna's travel experience would
lead to one of my own important life-defining moments.

A seed for travel had been planted.

~~~

My Nonno, Rocco "Rocky" D'Ammizio, was the patriarch of our
Italian family. An immigrant from Italy, he lived his life with a deep
appreciation and love for all he had: family, friends, and the joy of
being alive. He left a war-torn Italy in the late 1940s to start a new

life in Canada with his family. At one point during World War II in Italy, my Nonno had a German soldier hold a gun to his head, threatening his life.

My Nonno shared this emotional story with us while at the family dinner table one Sunday evening a few years ago. I can't recall what prompted his emotional monologue, but as soon as he began to speak, we concentrated on his words with curious anticipation.

The small village, where he was born and lived until his adult years, was infiltrated by the Germans, causing most of the town's residents to flee for safer pastures. My Nonno had fallen ill and remained in his home so he could rebuild strength for his escape, but his recovery hadn't come soon enough—they had reached his home. He tried to hide upstairs, but the soldiers found him and took him by the collar, shouting at him in German. With a gun to his head, he thought his life was over. He began to pray what he thought would be his final prayers on this earth. But for some reason, they halted their attack and quickly fled the building.

As he recounted his moments of fear and the threat of death, we felt paralyzed by his words. An eerie quietness fell over the room. He continued his story, and tears welled in his eyes as he described, by some fortunate miracle, how his life was spared.

He wasn't sure why he was so lucky to have been given his life back, but because of this defining moment, he lived every single day with unconditional gratitude.

That was the first and only time I heard that story.

My Nonno's gratitude for life was one that both my brother and I embraced, partly because of my Nonno's beautiful example. We loved life and felt blessed with our family. With gratitude comes happiness, and in general, I grew up content. I was thankful for the opportunities given to me through education, and later on with my career as a wedding planner.

Yes, I was happy, but as I grew older, I noticed something was missing. At the time, I couldn't put my finger on it as to why, but soon my life would be propelled in an entirely new direction.

~~~

The journey to discovering that "why" began as any other workday. It was late morning on a bleak December day, and I was coordinating the final preparations for a four-hundred person wedding to be held that evening. I was tired from a hectic work week and feeling oddly unsettled. I made the effort to shake it off and continue, running around in my four-inch stilettos (that also doubled as a great calf workout), when I received the phonecall that would change my life.

I'd returned to my office to administer a gentle foot massage and relax for a few minutes (perhaps indulging in some celebrity gossip websites to see what high-jinx had occurred that morning), when I noticed my phone flashing with eight missed calls. As I was about to check my messages, the phone rang again. On the other end was my dad, greeting me with an uncomfortable quietness in his voice. He never called me at work, so I instinctively knew something was very wrong.

I braced myself as he took extra time and care selecting his next words: Nonno had just had a serious stroke and was in the emergency room. Frozen by his words, my breath stopped and every muscle in my body tensed. Shock was something I'd never felt before. The reality of the situation finally caught up with my mind, and tears welled in my eyes. Without hesitation, I fled work, leaving the wedding in the hands of my assistant, and rushed to be by my Nonno's side.

By way of pure misfortune, everyone else in my family was out of town. When I arrived at the hospital, I was completely alone. My dad had been unable to meet me because he had to take care of my Nonna, whose advanced Alzheimer's required her to have full-time supervision. The emergency room would have been too much for her to handle. I arrived to find my Nonno, the strongest man I'd ever known, lying in a state I wish no one would ever have to experience.

Although unable to speak, he could open his eyes, so I held his hand and maintained eye contact with him to let him know I was there. A desperate sadness filled his eyes. It was as though he was crying without shedding tears. The intense worry and fear he expressed through his eyes shook me to my core, to my soul. It seemed like everything else around us was in slow motion. As difficult as it was, I knew I had to gather all the strength I could and send it to him. This was my Nonno, my rock. Could this really be happening? Until my family arrived, I held his hand, talked to him, and prayed with him.

A few days later, the doctors told us the devastating reality of the situation: he would never fully recover. Right there, at that moment, I lost a part of myself.

~ ~ ~

A few weeks before my Nonno's stroke, life had begun to unravel around me. After years of struggling with the decision, my mother announced she was separating from my father. Unfortunately, I knew this was a long time coming. She'd been talking to me openly about it for months, citing incidents that had been compounding over the years. But no matter how old you are, the breakup of your parents is troubling and difficult to move past. I knew that in the long run, it was the right decision, but when I was experiencing the initial repercussions of their choice, my heart saddened at the thought. Even though I didn't overtly express my grief at the end of my once picture-perfect family, anxiety was rising within me.

The mounting stress of my parents' issues, my Nonno in the hospital, and the heavy demands at work weighed me down. I couldn't sleep, yet wanted to sleep all the time. I was functioning on pure anxiety. Then one morning, I received a call from my dad—from the hospital. I braced myself for more unthinkable news about my

Nonno, only this time, he presented me with new devastating news: he too was admitted to the hospital after suffering a heart attack.

I was living in a haze of disbelief and monumental concern for my family who I used to think was invincible. How could this all be happening at once? And why?

The content life I'd been living faded away. From then on, I found it difficult to offer anyone a genuine smile. My moments of happiness went from infrequent to none at all. I couldn't even remember the things that made me happy. I was deflated. Simply existing.

I went through the motions at work, feeling listless and out of control. For the next week, I spent every evening at the hospital, visiting my dad on floor five and my Nonno on floor two. Then I'd go home, wrap myself in a blanket on the couch, and cry. I didn't know what else to do.

There was some relief from that exhausting routine when, thankfully, my dad's health improved and he was given the okay to return home for the rest of his recovery. But damage had already been done to my well-being and it began to affect my work.

As a wedding planner, I expelled an exhausting amount of energy to matters such as cake-cutting fees, seating arrangements, centrepieces, or any other detail which, to me, paled in comparison to the stress and heartache of seeing my Nonno slowly die. The happiness I brought to my job was replaced by hollowness. I stopped caring.

But the worst was still to come.

After three agonizing months in the hospital, my Nonno finally succumbed to his stroke.

I distinctly remember the moments before he passed. I studied every inch of his skin—his nails, his hands, his bushy eyebrows, his bald head—while he still had life and warmth in his body. When the doctors told us he had only minutes left, my family and I gathered around him. We braced ourselves as we placed a hand on his arms and, for the final time, felt the warmth of his soul. Together, we cried, waited, and counted every breath he took, each more laboured than the last. Then, the inevitable happened. He exhaled his last breath. My beloved Nonno was gone.

To be with a person as they breathe their last breath—that poignant moment when the soul is transferred from this world to the next—is definitive, yet surreal. This wasn't a bad dream though. It happened. I watched one of the greatest people I'd ever known die right before my eyes. My life was changed. In a few short months, everything that was familiar to me had dissolved, and I felt broken.

I went back to work a few days later and struggled. How would I even begin to adjust to living in a world that my Nonno was no longer in? I questioned myself and everything I was doing. Was I happy before or was I just assuming the role I'd fallen into? Could I be happy once again? What the hell was I going to do?

Often, it takes an event beyond our control to look back at our lives and re-evaluate. It could be a death, a lay-off, a break up, an accident—something that happens externally that manifests into an internal revelation, leading us to make a change.

With my Nonno's passing, my re-evaluation process had begun.

LIFE LESSON ONE:
SET BIG GOALS

*"The greater danger for most of us is not that our aim is too high
and we miss it, but that it is too low and we reach it."*
—Michelangelo

Before my Nonno's passing, I'd thought I was on the right track. I had a decent job and was thriving in my work community. I had weekly sales targets I continually surpassed. But these were the only goals I had in my life, and they were set for me by someone else. Without really thinking about it, I focused my attention on them while filling the rest of my life with white noise.

Now, without my Nonno, everything I thought was safe and whole had been altered, and something in my heart shifted. Something inside me longed for more. I knew these feelings of unrest weren't just symptoms of the pain I'd felt over the past few months. My intuition was telling me something. What was that something? I didn't know, but I made it my mission to figure it out. Journaling was my outlet.

I purchased the perfect journal, decorated with ornate colours and whimsical shapes, as the palette for my brainstorming exercise. It, of course, needed to be fancy. I began right away. Every night before bed I set aside time for myself to reflect and allow my thoughts to flow out. I wrote about how much I missed Nonno.

I wrote about how my family life had changed. I wrote down any thoughts and feelings that bubbled to the surface. I continued on with my mission, analyzing my written thoughts, and realized something very important was missing in my life: Inspiration.

Nothing big or awesome was happening. I coasted through my routine and let time pass without any real inspiring moments. It made me realize how complacent I felt at my job and how I wasn't aiming towards any bigger purpose. I had already reached my plateau.

This rattled me to my core. I needed to shake it off. In an attempt to elevate my spirits, I wrote down the questions I was trying to answer: What did I really want? What interested me, inspired me, and excited me? What was I was truly and unequivocally passionate about? In order to figure out the answers to these questions, I created a "wish list" of spectacular things I wanted to design for my life.

I brainstormed freely, openly, and with love. I didn't hold back what I wanted to accomplish or edit my aspirations because they seemed unreachable. There was no filter, only pure, raw dreams. I let myself dream as big as I possibly could and wrote down what would result in happiness. Ideas, images, and words raced through my mind! I began to feel really excited about putting to paper all of these magnificent ideas. This was so much fun!

Through this process, my innermost passions and joys were finally coming to the surface. Engaging in this creative exercise stirred up feelings of hope and excitement. I felt like I could breathe again after being suffocated for months by sadness. I actually felt happy. I'd never given myself the chance to explore my desires to such an extent before. Ideas ran through me like it was a divine purpose. I needed to follow my passions.

I narrowed it down further. The more I focused on my passions, the more I realized that everything intersected with travel and experiencing other cultures. A curiosity for travel had evolved from being an active listener to my Nonno and Nonna's tales of Mexican living to an adult wanting to explore the world. I wanted to create my own travel tales.

As I sifted through the pages in my journal, another realization came to light: I wanted to write. I had unintentionally suppressed my creative side since high school. I stopped painting and writing. I stopped being that artistic, imaginative girl I once was. How did I let my creativity—something that filled me with so much happiness—slip away?

Now was my chance to get it back. Then I thought: *Why not fuse the two passions together?* It was my time to do just that.

I boldly wrote down a huge, ridiculous, and awesome goal: *By November, I will be on the other side of the Pacific Ocean.* This was only four months away. I closed my eyes and visualized myself on a white sandy beach, journal in hand, and a smile stretched across my face. I pictured myself writing feverishly, my travels providing me with inspiration that would pour through my writing. I set the goal that my experiences would somehow inspire others to pursue their own dreams and live life with happiness.

But there was more—an even bigger goal: *I will write a book.* It felt right—like a memory waiting to happen. I had no idea how I was going to do that, nor what the content would be. And was I even qualified to write a book? Really, who did I think I was? I threw caution to the wind and put it out to the universe. And for the first time in months, I felt a fire ignite within me.

Through these new-found plans to travel and tap into my creative side, I began to unleash a better version of myself—the Ang I'd been missing the past few months, and maybe even longer than that. I loved that Ang! I needed to find her again.

~ ~ ~

I became obsessed with this new mission. Each night after work, I revisited the journal entry and smiled at the sight of my written goals. This exercise had enkindled a spark in my subconscious mind that guided my thoughts on a day-to-day basis. When I woke up in the morning and got ready for work, I'd catch myself daydreaming about different places I wanted to travel. When I had some down time between planning weddings, I searched different travel blogs for inspiration and answers to the curious thoughts I had about backpacking. My goals were like an invisible force gracefully pushing me in a distinct direction.

But, how could I do this when I felt so committed to my clients at work? How could I leave?

Unbeknownst to me, the universe had already set plans in motion that would contribute to the next step. So, when I was called into my manager's office one sunny September day, I had no idea what was coming.

~ ~ ~

"Ang, I'm really sorry, but we are laying you off."

My manager's words slapped me in the face. I asked him to repeat himself because I thought someone was playing a cruel joke on me. When he said it the second time, it felt like someone had punched me in the stomach. It didn't make any sense. I was wedding planner, extraordinaire! I was killing it at my job!

He explained how the economic downturn had affected my place of employment, and this was the start of a series of layoffs.

Why was I first? Why me?

I was angry, embarrassed, and, above everything else, sad. Tears streamed down my face as the reality of the situation sank in. After a few painfully awkward moments of me crying in front of my boss, he asked me if I needed a ride home. That was my subtle cue to exit his office and move on.

I charged back to my office and took the five hundred business cards I'd just ordered and chucked them into the garbage. "I guess I won't be needing these anymore!" I shouted at my computer screen. I picked up my purse, my fancy pen, and three reusable water bottles, and for the last time, walked out of my office.

That night, I ordered a large pizza with extra cheese and blue cheese dipping sauce, and wallowed in my sadness. I allowed myself to feel depressed about my job situation for precisely 48 hours. During that time, I'd called friends, and through lengthy conversations rationalized all the reasons why I was the company's number one employee and how they'd made the biggest mistake in history. I tried to debate about the economic situation (which I had zero insight on), I got angry, and I even name-called.

And then, I understood.

The universe had been listening with open ears to that big, lofty goal I had set for myself and was presenting me with an obvious escape route.

It was decided. I was going to travel and I was going to write.

A controlled presence entered my life the second I made the decision. I felt power, strength, and courage. I was on the cusp of something monumental. I knew I was about to embark on experiences that would change me. I knew I was going to take in everything with an open mind and a loving heart.

And in making that decision, I took the first step in transforming into the person I wanted to be. Someone I am proud of. Someone who is truly happy.

Then, I did what any other person would do at a major life crossroad. I drank a bottle of wine and booked a one-way ticket to Thailand set to leave three weeks later. Was it the most rational decision? No. Had I prepared financially for it? Absolutely not. Did I go to the bank and shamefully increase the limit of my credit card? Yes. Was I ready for my life to take a dramatically radical turn in a new and exciting direction? Oh, hell yes!

The plan was already in motion and the countdown was on. From that moment of creating goals, my life was forever changed and soon propelled me on the path to living the life of my dreams.

SET BIG GOALS

I once read a beautifully simplistic quote that said, "It's a dream until you write it down, then it is a goal." When you write goals down, your accountability becomes real. You have direction.

Goals with specific measures allow directional focus on what exactly you want to spend your time and energy on. A goal acts as your funnel, which guides and channels your efforts effectively into your desired outcome.

When you don't have goals, you allow yourself to float around your every day. Goals draw together the larger scope of your life. They're something to drive and motivate you to greater accomplishments. Goals contain a silent force that, if you continue to follow their fundamental encouragement, can bring more definitive purpose to a complacent life. They serve as constant motivational reminders and help you achieve your highest potential. Most of all, goals allow you to grow as a person.

CALL TO ACTION

Think about what you want to achieve and why it's important to you. Your goals present your inner desires. What do you want to create in your life? What is your big, awesome, ridiculous goal, where the very thought of achieving it gives you butterflies?

Determine what fills you with excitement and happiness and how you can point all those things to one target.

1. **Be specific.** The more you define your goal, the clearer the path will be to achieving it.

2. **Write it down.**

3. **Visualize** your goal and keep that as a guiding force.

4. ***Take action.*** Do something today that will help you move closer to your goal. It could be as simple as reading an article about someone who has done something similar or registering for a class that provides the tools you need to achieve it.

No matter how big or small the action, keep the momentum going and move forward.

LIFE LESSON TWO:
FORGIVE AND LET GO

"In the middle of difficulty lies opportunity."
—Albert Einstein

The three weeks leading to my departure were a blur. I had a million things to prepare, but was clueless about where to start. Finally, I decided to begin with daily visits to the local bookstore to research and jot down points from Lonely Planet and Frommer's travel guidebooks about backpacking in Thailand. I figured that was a good place to start.

Also worth noting: I'm not a backpacking kind of girl. I enjoy fancy glasses of wine, designer clothing, and luxurious accommodations. The finer things in life. So roughing it, as I was planning to do, was going to be a pretty big challenge.

The day before I left, I worked on my travel blog, simply titled, "Ang's Adventures Abroad." I needed an outlet for the creative writing I'd committed to, and a trendy blog seemed like the perfect fit. I sat in the nest of clothes that should have already been packed and brainstormed ideas to include in my inaugural post. After narrowing my thoughts down, I knew the first post had to be about the packing process and my inevitable associated challenges.

How on earth was I going to consolidate all of my material possessions and necessities into one backpack? True, it was the Cadillac of backpacks, but I'm a girl who packs three pairs of stilettos for an overnight slumber party with the girls, "just in case."

I also wasn't quite sure how the backpack actually worked. As I was packing, I continued to find additional magical compartments and sections that broke off from the original backpack for more compact travel. I was beyond confused. It seemed far too high-tech for my travel plans. I recorded all of these complex thoughts and translated them into a witty blog post.

After approximately four hours of shifting between packing, calling friends, checking Facebook, napping, rolling around in the nest of clothes, and writing a blog post, I was packed and ready to go. I waited for that feeling of excitement, the way I'd felt when I booked my trip to Thailand. But it wasn't quite there. In fact, I felt a bit skittish and itchy in my skin. Something was bothering me. Although I had made all these sweeping movements towards my dreams, something was weighing me down.

I sat on the floor, trying to quiet my anxious mind and figure out what the problem was. After a few moments, my mind slowed down and narrowed in on the weight. It was anger. It still lingered from being laid-off at work.

During the weeks of preparation for my trip, I hadn't dealt with being thrust into unemployment. I'd skirted my angry thoughts by filling my mind with excitement. That was awesome and all, but now, as I prepared to say goodbye to Canada, feelings of anger, sadness, insecurity, and humiliation bubbled back to the surface. Yes, I was on the path to doing something great, but I was still mad. Really effing mad.

Those jerks had undermined the great work I'd done for the company and were willing to let me go. How was I so easily dispensable when I had proved myself time and time again? How could I not take this personally? An overwhelming feeling of embarrassment came over me, which fueled my anger.

I spiraled into a pit of resentment. Tears welled in my eyes. In a matter of moments, I'd gone from being excited about Thailand to being stuck in the hurt of being laid-off. What the hell? I absolutely did not want to feel like this! Something had to change. *I* had to change. So I let out one final cry, punched a pillow, and made the decision to move on.

I needed to forgive, and most importantly, I needed to let go of my anger.

Letting go of anger for me wasn't like switching off a light. Deciding to forgive, however, was the most important first step in moving forward. I had to detach myself from the negative emotions I felt towards those who had made me feel dispensable and unimportant. My travels were supposed to be connected to the positive intentions I had set for myself.

I was annoyed that my anger was affecting my excitement. Screw that. I deserved to be excited! I consciously chose not to allow their decision to lay me off, which I had no control over, define me. By focusing on the incident, I gave it power. I allowed it to create a greater and unwanted negative force in my life. What I *did* have control over was my ability to forgive and let go.

I let it go—that suffocating moment of anger and shock I was stuck in—and instantly felt relieved. I was able to once again focus on that awesome feeling of excitement—I was on the brink of something incredible. In a few hours I'd board a plane and travel to the other side of the world. I had an infinite number of opportunities ahead of me.

There was so much I wanted to create, and I knew I had the capacity to do so, if only I let go. So I did. When I look back at the experience surrounding my former job, I can see how it led me to shape my life the way I wanted: free and ready for the journey of a lifetime.

FORGIVE AND LET GO

Forgiveness is not about the other person. Forgiveness is about you.

Embarking on my journey with a chip on my shoulder wasn't going to affect anyone at my former workplace. It was only going to affect me.

Did I want to feel palpable resentment weighing over me as I pranced along the beaches of Thailand? Oh, hell no! I wanted to be free of the hurt I'd been holding in. I had an amazing opportunity in front of me and I wanted to embrace it with love.

By reliving the events of despair, you inflict suffering on yourself. When you hold on to a grudge, it consumes you with negative thoughts. Letting go of those feelings doesn't mean you condone what happened. It just means the past will no longer affect your present or future.

If past resentment occupies space in your mind, it prevents you from filling that space with new opportunities and focusing on things you do want to create. When you release your grip on something you can't change, you give yourself power to move on. It happened, and now it's in the past. The important next step is to move forward.

No one wants to be angry, but for some reason, we hold onto it because we think the other person doesn't deserve our forgiveness. And that justifies our anger. This life lesson encourages you to distance yourself from this default setting and take the bold move to forgive and let go. You'll be able to feel closure and be at peace. Release your anger with a genuine intention of forgiveness and see how your energy shifts. In letting go of negativity, you're brought closer to happiness.

CALL TO ACTION

Are you holding onto something that brings you feelings of inadequacy, anger, or worse? Are you holding onto a grudge? Is there something that brings you a feeling of unsettlement and anxiety? It's time to let that anger go.

> *Practice forgiveness.* Say aloud, "I forgive you," while directing your thoughts towards that person or situation. Your mind will catch up with your words.

Let go. This is the most difficult step as this action comes in various forms. It could take place as a symbolic action, such as writing down your resentful thoughts on a piece of paper and throwing it into a fire. It could be writing your sorrows in the sand and allowing the waves to wash them away. It could even be letting out your frustrations by punching a pillow like I did. Screaming at the top of your lungs for a few minutes also works.

Allow a release. These actions are a step forward in moving on, and even though the action may be small, it triggers momentum to push you forward into feeling free.

LIFE LESSON THREE: LET GO OF YOUR LIST

"Courage is the power to let go of the familiar."
— Raymond Lindquist

While Thailand tops the destination list for many backpackers, I have a first degree connection to the country: my aunt and uncle own an apartment there. This was perfect for me, a person most would consider the antithesis of a backpacker. I'd have somewhere other than a hostel (a standard accommodation for a backpacker) to stay. Score!

Aunt Josie, my mom's sister, and her husband, Uncle Andre, moved to Southeast Asia in the early 1990s. Having achieved teaching success in their careers in Canada, they decided to take on an adventure and teach overseas. Their wanderlust was directly correlated to my Nonno and Nonna's desire to travel. Aunt Josie and Uncle Andre didn't just want to travel, they wanted to completely immerse themselves in another culture. They started in Brunei, a tiny country on the island of Borneo.

I remember receiving letters describing their adventures of dinners at the local yacht club or treks through the jungles and, my favourite in particular, nights at the Sultan of Brunei's palace. They saw monkeys on their way to work, and geckos were familiar and friendly houseguests. Oh, and it was always warm (cue tan envy).

15

On their breaks from school (which seemed awesomely long and often), they flew to neighbouring countries such as Vietnam, Indonesia, and Thailand. Even though they were on the other side of the world and I missed them dearly, I loved their lifestyle and couldn't help but brag about their experiences as they were exotic beyond my comprehension. First my grandparents, then my aunt and uncle. The desire for travel was ingrained in me.

After 10 years in Brunei, Aunt Josie and Uncle Andre purchased an apartment outside the bustling capital of Thailand, Bangkok, to serve as a hub and a motivator to continue their travels. When the time came, they offered me the use of the apartment.

I reflected on Aunt Josie and Uncle Andre's motivations to travel: not only to seek adventure and culture, but also to let go of their list of anything that chipped away at their happiness. It got me thinking about the way we regulate our lives based on lists we create—lists of our fears, lists of people, places, and things we don't like, lists of grudges we hold onto. We stop ourselves from taking action because of the barriers we construct.

I knew that once I shed my layer of anger, I'd have a few other things to let go of in order to be open during my travels. I had a very specific list of likes and dislikes, "hang-ups" if you will, that shaped how I approached life. A common saying amongst my friends begins with, "Ang Urquhart does not..." or "Ang Urquhart loves...". The list of items to follow my name includes, but is not limited to...

Ang Urquhart does not:

- wait in lines;
- like Frisbees;
- like bees;
- enjoy early mornings;
- swim in deep water with fish; or
- eat anything with "shelf-life" (I obsessively check food best before dates).

Ang Urquhart loves:

- Beyoncé;
- being fancy;
- when people scream laugh;
- movie trailers, no matter the movie;
- when people clap in a circle; and
- nachos. Period.

The list was a tad ridiculous (but also a touch hilarious). During my forthcoming travels, I'd be faced with circumstances that might cross the boundaries of my comfort and tolerance zone. So, I needed to go in carte-blanche. I wanted to focus on and appreciate the simple pleasures and quirky events the world would present to me. When Aunt Josie and Uncle Andre let go, they were rewarded with fabulous overseas adventures and regular encounters with monkeys.

What I deemed necessary to move forward was to let go of the "Ang does not" column and focus on love. I didn't want to be stuck in negative energy, hanging on to those limiting thoughts could potentially filter to other areas of my life. To embrace the open mind and loving heart stance, I had to let go of my negative list.

Once I let go of the insignificant hang-ups, I created a new and exciting energy. I made the agreement not to let my little idiosyncrasies hold me back or hinder my thinking. Letting go of my list was a mandatory life lesson before setting off overseas.

I let go of my list and was open to create a new bucket list of love, of things that would shape my travels in ways I couldn't have ever imagined. I let go of my list and felt instantly free.

LET GO OF YOUR LIST

Sometimes we hold onto ideas so long we don't realize they're holding us back. We become comfortable with our restrictive lists, which can transform into a character trait. A list item could begin as a fear of Frisbees, but grow into a fear of trying something new.

Letting go of your "I do not like…" column and instead replacing it with "I love…" statements catapults you into a position of gratitude.

CALL TO ACTION

Reserve some time to check in with yourself and observe any of your quirks, high-maintenance hang-ups, and even things you dislike. Grab a pen and paper and write them down.

Here's where the real work comes into play:

Take a moment to study your list. Ask yourself, "Do these hang-ups contribute to living the best version of myself or do they hold me back or limit me in some way?"

Identify what the positive outcome will be. For example, if you dislike early mornings, you can focus, instead, on the extra time you gain by waking up early, which provides more time to be productive and sets the tone for a positive day.

Next, extract the top three items on your list that you want to focus on, then ask yourself, "If I let go of these hang-ups, what would the positive end result be?"

Write down the positive result next to each hang-up.

By letting go of your negatives, you create space for the possibility of something pretty damn awesome to take its place. The space created can now be filled with a list of loves or positive end results. Focus your attention here and embrace the shift to a positive and open mindset.

LIFE LESSON FOUR:
CREATE A MANTRA

*"Whatever we plant in our subconscious mind and nourish with
repetition and emotion will one day become a reality."*
– Earl Nightingale

By 4:00 a.m. on my departure day (a cold and blustery November morning), I was ready to go. I'd finally completed packing my backpack, the only constant, tangible item I'd have for the next few months. As ready as I could be physically, I loaded the car with my belongings. My mom had offered to drive me to the airport, so as the sun rose, we made our way to Toronto Pearson International Airport.

I felt prepared. I had my backpack, passport, and travel documents organized and ready to go. I had all the "stuff" I needed. We pulled out of the driveway. This was it! This was when my life was going to change. But, as we merged onto the highway, my excitement somehow mutated into something unexpected.

What was this feeling? All of a sudden, I had an overwhelming urge to throw up or cry or scream or an epic combination of all three. What was happening?!

The reality and magnitude of what I was about to embark on hit me hard. Reality, doubt, and fear slammed into me, causing me to shake uncontrollably. What in God's name was I doing? How could

I just take off to a foreign country by myself? Who did I think I was? Panic set in, and I felt my heart trying to beat its way out of my chest. I was absolutely terrified.

I frantically instructed my mom to pull over to the side of the highway. My mind was racing with thoughts of fear and doubt. Did I have it in me to travel to the other side of the world alone? Is it too late to back out?

Up to that point, I had avoided the possible emotional ramifications of traveling solo to the other side of the world with no game plan. I had ignored dealing with the monumental moments cresting in my life—moments with the potential to be life-defining. Here was where thought and action intersected, and I needed to shift my energy accordingly. I took a deep breath in through my nose and let a long exaggerated sigh out of my mouth to bring myself back to the present moment. I needed to do something to elevate my spirits back to courage and excitement.

I needed to create a mantra.

I'm a huge fan of the book, "The Secret," which is based on the Law of Attraction. This law is rooted in the notion that we attract whatever we think about, good or bad. I abide by this and believe we're all involved in an exchange with the energy around us on the planet and beyond.

I needed to lift my current emotional state to a more optimistic level, which required positive energy. I knew I had to tap into this universal energy source to channel the strength I had within. Because my goal was to be the best version of myself, I created a personal mission statement, or mantra, to help me get there.

The term mantra originates from ancient India and is found in Hinduism, Buddhism, and Jainism teachings. The action of a mantra focuses on sound and the vibrations that exist in the universe through the practice of chanting. Mantras, which consist of a single sound or a series of sounds, are charged with a psycho-spiritual power that empowers the mind in an almost magical way. A mantra is used as a tool to attract desirable ideas, experiences, and people into your life.

As I sat in the car on the side of the highway, in an effort to distance myself from my fears and my doubts, I created a short statement—a few powerful words to change my headspace and direct my mindset to focus on this trip and beyond.

I am a strong, brave woman with an open mind and a loving heart, living the best version of myself.

On my way to the airport, the most important idea within my mantra was bravery. I had the strength to confront my fears and feelings of doubt.

I am a strong, brave woman.

It reinforced the agreement with myself to approach challenges and new experiences with a receptive and loving stance. I chose to be open to new opportunities and embrace what Thailand, and wherever else my travels would take me, had to offer. I would bring awareness to my choices along the way and allow love to emanate through my actions.

By creating that mantra, I reaffirmed my motivations as to why I wanted to embark on these travels: to find my happiness. I wanted to emerge a stronger person from the challenges I had faced. When I truly thought about it, I realized I was incredibly strong and brave for going on these travels. I had already embraced the mindset of an open mind and loving heart. I was already on the path of living the best version of myself.

I repeated my mantra at least a dozen times aloud, and with that I could feel that spark of joy creep back into my heart. "Okay, let's do this!" I shouted to my mom, who had quietly (and without judgment) observed me through my mantra chanting process. She merged back onto the highway, laughing and talking with her Dramatically Zen daughter all the way to the airport.

I said goodbye to my mom, hoisted my monstrosity of a backpack over my shoulders, and slowly walked into the airport ready to launch on my travels. I decided to make that moment 25 points more dramatic by turning on my iPod and blasting the classic song, *Don't Stop Believin'* by Journey. I took a deep breath, recited my mantra to myself once more, and with absolute conviction and a smile across my face, made my way through airport customs.

CREATE A MANTRA

Through mantras, the universe hears the message you send out in a repetitive and positive fashion and, by saying these words with conviction, your requests will be answered.

When you're faced with moments of uncertainty and self-doubt, create a customized mantra. Use positive language, repeat what you desire to create in your life and feel confident that those results will happen. Repetition reinforces your positive words, causing you to move past whatever aspect of doubt or fear you may have. It then propels you into a new positive space.

CALL TO ACTION

How do you want to direct your mindset? Look within. Once you determine your goals, transform them into a mantra.

Begin a mantra by completing the sentence, "I AM..."
These two words are infused with power, and you can elevate your entire energy by beginning your sentence with this.

I AM strong. I AM intelligent. I AM happy.

Chant the words aloud.

Repeat. Soon, you'll feel these statements resonate within you.

LIFE LESSON FIVE: BE POSITIVE IN THE PRESENT

"Change your thoughts and you change your world."
—*Norman Vincent Peale*

After a 27-hour flight from Toronto to Thailand, I finally arrived at the Suvarnabhumi International Airport in Bangkok. Traveling in economy class for such a long flight wasn't how I would have chosen to fly if money wasn't a factor. It's my belief I should be in first class at all times, being fancy and sipping champagne. But really though, what kind of backpacker would I be had I flown in first class?

Needless to say, I did not enjoy the torturous flight from Toronto to Bangkok in economy.

I'll mention this fact about myself now. When I get anxious, I have insomnia so bad not even my doctor-prescribed sleeping pills can knock me out. I attempted to sleep during the 11-hour connecting flight from Vancouver to Tokyo, but was unsuccessful, so I took a little magic blue sleeping pill. The combination of excitement, anticipation, and disbelief from being en route to Asia kept my mind racing. I became engulfed in a bizarre half-entranced, half-awake state, with my exhaustion exponentially increasing.

I reached a point of discomfort I could no longer bear during the connecting flight from Tokyo to Bangkok. After almost two days,

I hadn't logged a single hour of sleep. I was exhausted, restless and, much to my dismay, seated beside a person who smelled slightly of chicken noodle soup and mistook me for a body pillow. After nearly one-third of an entire day trapped spooning with a stranger, I finally reached Bangkok with a monumental sense of relief and happiness to be off that plane.

That happiness, however, was only temporary.

I lightly jogged over to the luggage terminal and eagerly awaited my beloved backpack, excited to begin my travels. My anticipation grew as I observed other passengers collecting their belongings and happily heading out. The crowd around me became increasingly smaller, with less and less luggage on the carousel. My heart beat faster as the crowd dwindled even further. Something was wrong. My excitement quickly turned into panic as I realized my backpack was missing.

With my sleep deprivation, I'd stumbled so close to delirium that I wasn't sure if my mind was playing tricks or if this was actually happening. Jet lag plays a villain in my life whenever I travel as my internal body clock is extremely sensitive to it. A short trip to Chicago, which is only a one-hour time difference from where I live in Canada, thrusts me into a disheveled tizzy for a week. With a 12-hour time difference in Thailand, I was one shade away from disaster. With my exhaustion compounding atop my missing backpack, I did what I tend to do in moments of stress. I cried.

What came next was unexpected. Mid-cry, a timeless quote from Maya Angelou popped into my mind, "I've learned that you can tell a lot about a person by the way she handles these three things: a rainy day, lost luggage, and tangled Christmas tree lights."

That was all I needed to step back and reassess. I reconnected with the mantra I'd created earlier: *I am a strong, brave woman with an open mind and a loving heart, living the best version of myself.*

Saying this grounded me and stopped the tears, and I was able to move forward and calmly explain my situation to the airport staff.

After 20 minutes of *trying* to communicate with the only three Thai words I knew: hello; Bangkok; and Singha Beer, (which weren't helpful at all) and using large, dramatic hand gestures, I realized that nothing would be solved that late at night. The best (and really, the only) option was to return in the morning. An odd sense of clarity came over me, and I knew I had to let go of the negative situation temporarily. I had to keep moving forward.

I walked out of the airport with the tiniest of tiny carry-on bags I could've packed for myself (in retrospect, a poor idea) and felt complete trust in the first cab driver who approached me, directing him to take me to the nearest hotel (another poor and probably unsafe idea). I arrived 30 minutes later to what I would consider a one-star hotel in the middle of an industrial park, questioning if it was actually the nearest hotel. My exhaustion engulfing me, I collapsed on the bed and released the day.

The next morning, I returned to the airport, confident I'd be reunited with my backpack, but my belongings were still nowhere to be found. I felt a glimmer of hope, though, when I saw another backpack similar to mine in the holding area from my flight. I deduced that someone had mistakenly taken my backpack, thinking it was theirs, and would be coming soon to return it. If this person was indeed backpacking through Thailand as I suspected, why would they keep a backpack that wasn't theirs? I banked on them coming back to get the right one. Since it was out of my hands, there was no use sulking about it.

Hey, I was in Thailand! I put on my positive bravado and decided to attack the day. And somehow, I had a feeling everything would work out.

Maya Angelou would be proud of my next move: I celebrated my arrival—I was half way around the world in Thailand and my life was pretty damn awesome. Since I didn't have any luggage, I walked across the street to the gorgeous Novotel Hotel. Why and how didn't I see this the night before? I knew I belonged in this hotel and, more importantly, in the pool area.

I quickly called on my acting skills from grade 11 drama class and pretended to wave to a friend across the lobby, before casually sauntering past the front desk and into the pool area. Mission accomplished! I rolled up my Lululemon pants, looped the bottom of my shirt through the top, creating a makeshift bikini top, and embraced the sun and my surroundings in this five-star pool.

With my recently practiced Thai language skills, I ordered a couple of Singha Beers and a plain cheese pizza for one (the cheese tasted different—salty and sweet at the same time). I reclined on my lounge chair, with a smile on my face and slice of pizza in hand.

As beautiful trickling water fountains, palm trees, and exotic flowers surrounded me, there was no possible way I could be stressed, worried, or angry. I loved life! It didn't matter that I'd had a mini panic-attack the previous day or that my luggage was still in limbo. I accepted my current situation and relished in my glorious surroundings.

After my afternoon of fun, I returned to the airport feeling jazzed about life and my pool experience. And, just as I had wished for, found my that backpack had been returned! I rejoiced with glee and kicked my feet up into my first Thailand cartwheel. In addition, the person who accidentally took my backpack left me a heartfelt apology note accompanied by his business card and, much to my welcomed surprise, US$50 for the inconvenience.

Actions like this reiterate my belief that in general, the majority of people have an inherent positive goodness. This fellow traveller didn't have a hidden agenda to disrupt my travel plans by taking my luggage. Mistakes happen, especially when extreme exhaustion plays a role. I could have either let myself stew over something out of my control or take a step back with a positive mindset, relax, and release it. Besides, I now had a story to tell and I was $50 richer!

Upon receipt of my precious backpack, I took a taxi cab (which, by the way was hot pink, so that's awesome) to my Aunt Josie and Uncle Andre's apartment, located about 30 minutes outside of downtown Bangkok. I settled in and then prepared to leave for the popular tourist destination Khao San Road. With my luggage returned and an extra $50 added to my travel fund, I embraced a wickedly positive mindset and properly began my journey!

BE POSITIVE IN THE PRESENT

Sometimes we miss the bigger picture when faced with adversity. Instead, we focus on the negativity of the immediate problem at hand. When frustrated, judgment and logical thinking become clouded, and we tend to make knee-jerk reactions. Those reactions can distance us from what we need to do to be successful.

After sneaking into the luxury hotel across the street, I was able to take stock of my situation and come up with a worst-case scenario and action plan for how to deal with it. If my backpack was never returned to me, I would have purchased the items I needed for my travels along the way. Hey, the worst-case scenario would have forced me to buy an entire new summer wardrobe, which wouldn't have been too shabby at all!

Even in the most grim of situations, there's a silver lining. This life lesson encourages you to seek out that silver lining. By focusing on the positive in the present moment, you resist the urge to time travel to past stress or future outcomes built on assumptions. You change the entire energy of a situation and can even change, what may feel like a grave experience, into an entertaining one.

CALL TO ACTION

Next time you're faced with a challenging situation, take a moment to weigh the various outcomes.

Ask yourself, "What is the worst-case scenario?"

Rate the severity of it on a scale from one to 10.

Visualize the worst-case scenario, then come up with solutions should you find yourself in that situation. Chances are, at least one solution is easily attainable.

Focus your attention on the final solution you've come up with and check into that spark of positivity and goodness that lies within you.

Practice optimism. By engaging in a positive stance over the negative one you may tend to default to, your spirits will be elevated immediately.

LIFE LESSON SIX: TALK TO STRANGERS

"There are no strangers here; only friends you haven't met."
—William Butler Yeats

After two days in Bangkok, I felt I had experienced all I needed to in the land-locked, bustling capital of Thailand. I visited the infamous Khao San Road twice, where I learned cocktails were vastly less expensive than in Canada (of which I took full advantage). I also discovered that I could acquire a university degree for only $10 and buy a wedding dress for $8.

The Road was an overwhelming spectacle of every perceived tourist desire and, while I embraced its enchantment, I was ready to move on. A beach was an urgent requirement . I walked to the nearest travel agency—which to my delight was also a deli, scarf shop, and massage parlour—and booked a flight across the country.

I emerged from the store with a one-way ticket to Phuket in one hand, and a cheese sandwich in the other. All in all, a successful visit.

As I settled in to my flight to Phuket, an island on the west coast of Thailand located in the Andaman Sea, my initial happiness morphed into worry. It dawned on me that I had no idea what to do or where to go once I arrived. I made the decision to let go of any agenda or restrictions I usually put in place, and instead simply go with the flow. This worked fine for the first two days of frolicking along the streets of Khao San Road, but I'd have to start making some decisions soon. There were countless different beaches and about a hundred hostels, guest houses, and hotels to choose from. But I had zero direction. None.

I was by myself with no plan and no idea where to go.

During the one-hour flight, I scanned the plane for people who looked cool, fun, and on a similar wavelength to mine. While waiting for my backpack on the luggage carousel, which I did with hawk eyes this time, I noticed a small group of people laughing and enjoying themselves. Based on their genuine smiles, I concluded they were nice people and my potential new friends.

I slowly inched closer to their conversation so I could be within earshot. Everything seemed like jokes and good times, so I took a step closer and echoed their laughter. My three soon-to-be friends looked over at me, eyebrows raised in confusion. In what seemed like the longest and most awkward moment, I waited for their reaction to my interruption. With a cheeky smile on my face, I broke the silence and introduced myself. They responded with their names: Jackie, John, and Rob.

So far, so good. They hadn't run in fear of my boldness or inappropriateness. The conversation picked up and flowed freely.

Jackie and John, a lovely couple from England, were on their first trip to Thailand to celebrate their anniversary. Aboard the flight, they sat next to Rob, a solo backpacker, also from England. During the short trip from Bangkok to Phuket, Jackie, John, and Rob went from being strangers to friends and had agreed to embark on their first coastal adventure in Thailand together.

They seemed to embody a Dramatically Zen open mind, loving heart perspective, and here I was fortunate enough to connect with them.

After about 10 minutes of witty repartee, we realized none of us knew where to go next and decided to explore Phuket together.

By breaking free from my social norms of home, not talking to strangers, I set into motion a series of events that would positively affect my travels for the next two weeks.

The four of us banded together to arrange our first beachside destination. We grabbed a few marketing pamphlets from the airport lobby about Phuket, and through collaborative research in the 30-minute van ride from the airport, we decided on Kata Beach. I was about to visit my first beach in Thailand! With friends! This was so exciting!

I could feel myself glowing on the inside and out as I realized I now had an infinite number of possibilities for my journey ahead. And this was only the third day.

TALK TO STRANGERS

When we were young, we were persistently told, "Don't talk to strangers." This made sense because bad people exist, and children aren't adept at discerning who they are. But our suspicion of strangers as children can shift into our adult lives. The self-preserving fear of bad people becomes a barrier that can prevent us from establishing relationships with good people.

Instead of carrying the fear that may have been imposed on as a child, this life lesson encourages you to be vulnerable and let that fear go. Apply an open mind, loving heart attitude and look for the goodness in others, instead of functioning under the assumption that they're bad. Let down your guard, push past your personal constraints and talk to strangers. This optimism towards something or someone unknown will bring forward an openness to new ideas and possibilities.

I believe that people are inherently nice and generally don't want to stifle this niceness. Because of this, the idea of talking to strangers is comforting to me, as there's a high possibility that I'll connect to that nice person and be well-received. It's very rare that someone you reach out to on a friendly level will react with hostility. By reaching out to someone new, you offer a moment of alliance, show kindness, and ultimately connect in the simplest way. Odds are, that kindness will be reciprocated. This may allow the other person to step out of their personal comfort zone too. You may even be a catalyst to someone else's personal growth.

Talking to a stranger can spice up a typically routine scenario. That small gesture of kindness or friendly conversation with the person next to you at the local Starbucks may make that person's day. Maybe they are someone who you see on a regular basis, but never took the moment to talk to because they were a stranger. Now, you've opened the door to becoming more than a stranger, rather an acquaintance or potentially a friend.

CALL TO ACTION

By opening up and adhering to this life lesson, you allow for the other person to open up as well.

Here are a few ways you can "talk to strangers" without teetering on the creepy side of the spectrum:

Smile and say hello.

Make eye contact.

Pay it forward or practice a random act of kindness. For example, let the person with fewer groceries go ahead you in line.

Start up a casual conversation with someone around you. The easiest conversation starter is commenting on the weather—everyone loves to talk about a sunny day!

Introduce yourself to that familiar face at your local coffee shop or bus stop.

The simple gesture of saying hello and coming from a friendly place can catapult you to a new level of comfort. You create the atmosphere for positivity to take place.

LIFE LESSON SEVEN: OFFER SIMPLE GREETINGS

"I will never understand all the good a simple smile can accomplish."
—Mother Teresa

Things were looking up! I was in Thailand, far away from the November coldness in Canada, and had new travel companions. After arriving at Kata Beach, we put our accommodation-seeking mission on hold to celebrate our new-found friendship over food. We selected a restaurant on the shoreline with front-row seats to view the crimson sun sinking below the horizon.

As we entered the restaurant, my friends lined up in a receiving-line fashion and bowed to the hostess greeting us. The hostess reciprocated, everyone smiling at the pleasantries.

I, on the other hand, was confused. I asked Jackie, "What just happened and how can I get in on that?"

She explained that they'd participated in the traditional Thai "Wai" greeting. Wai happens when you enter a building. A gracious Thai bows in front of you with hands clasped in prayer and declares, "Sawasdee Ka," which means hello.

Everywhere you go in Thailand, whether a café, a scarf/deli/ travel agency or even a temple, a moment is taken to recognize your arrival. There's a genuine effort to make sure your presence is not only recognized, but sincerely appreciated too.

This resonated with me, and I wanted to jump on the band-wagon immediately. I exited the restaurant, waited a moment, then re-entered so I could start fresh with my first Wai experience. The hostess laughed at my dramatics, bowed, and said "Sawasdee Ka." I followed suit, slowly bowing while relishing in the pleas-ant exchange.

As I completed my bow, I directed my energy towards the hostess. She smiled warmly back. I loved it! Wow! I had no idea something so simple could bring such joy. Practicing the Wai acknowledgment triggered an unsuspected high level of happiness within me, so I figured there must be something to these simple greetings.

When I joined my friends at our dinner table, they'd already ordered us drinks served in pineapples (I loved these people already). As I took a sip of my sugary cocktail loaded with four shots of unidentifiable liquor, I thought about other simple greetings already in place in my life.

I never understood a word of Italian mass when I went to church with my Nonno and Nonna, but I always looked forward to the end when we gave others seated around us the sign of peace. The language barrier didn't mean anything because the action simply focused on shaking another person's hand. It always conjured up emotions of joy. Even at a young age, I recognized the benefits. I constantly got butterflies of happiness after participating in this ritual.

The more I thought about it, the more I realized North America has a number of these greetings too. Have you ever heard of the "Jeep wave," where people who drive a Jeep give each other a little nod when passing the other on the road? It's another form of a simple greeting—an understanding between two strangers who give one another a shout out. My brother has a Jeep and participates in this social contract. I remember the first time I witnessed the wave, I chuckled at the action. I soon realized it was a courtesy extended to someone sharing common ground. In that case, owning a jeep. How basic, yet how awesome. Now when I'm there to experience it, I'm brought to all sorts of levels of happiness.

And one of my favourite simple greetings is the "cottage wave" that takes place, well, you guessed it—at the cottage. The action specifically occurs when you wave at those passing by on a boat while you sit on the dock, or vice versa. The objective of this small gesture is to exchange friendliness with others who share the cottage experience. You make a small connection that not only makes you feel good, but makes the other person feel pretty damn good as well. And again, solidifies my belief that people are inherently awesome.

The sun had set and my first meal on the west coast of Thailand was complete. As we exited the restaurant, the hostess once again bowed and said, "Sawasdee Ka," which also meant goodbye. Like choreography, my travel crew and I bowed with hands clasped in prayer form, leaving the restaurant slightly drunk and entirely elated.

OFFER SIMPLE GREETINGS

When you acknowledge the goodness in others and send out a form of loving kindness through a simple greeting, you receive that goodness too. In doing so, you send out gratitude and positive energy, moving forward with good vibes.

We're all linked in some way and, by offering a simple greeting and recognizing our interconnectedness, we are contributing to a friendlier and happier way of living.

CALL TO ACTION

You don't need to drive a Jeep or own a cottage to infuse simple greetings into your everyday life.

Here are some examples of how to participate:

Smile at the next person walking by.

Give a courtesy wave to another driver who lets you in their lane or offers you some sort of driver-to-driver courtesy.

Write a warm salutation in emails to set a positive tone.

Acknowledge a customer service representative by name. Servers and retailers usually wear name tags.

Smile as you say hello when answering the phone. I swear you can hear the smile in your voice.

It only takes a quick second to extend some graciousness to another person, and you almost always feel good in return.

LIFE LESSON EIGHT: RECITE DAILY AFFIRMATIONS

"I figured that if I said it enough, I would convince the world that I really was the greatest."
– Muhammed Ali

$\mathcal{F}$ollowing our delightful dinner in Phuket, my travel crew and I finally decided it was time to determine where to bunk, so we explored the narrow streets of Kata, our new home for the next little while. As we meandered our way through the quaint coastal town, I could hear the rhythmic sounds of the waves crashing against the shore in the background. I felt an exhilarating awakening as I breathed in the fresh sea air. I had to pinch myself. Was I really there?

Ten minutes into our search, we happened upon a collection of guesthouses cascading down a palm tree-lined hill overlooking the beach. The best part was that it was a mere CA$25 per night to stay! The bungalows were brand new and complete with refrigerators, king-sized beds, air conditioners, large mirrors, bath robes and flat screen TVs—a huge score!

One quick side note: Since all three of my new friends were British, it was taking everything in my power not to speak with an accent.

Overjoyed by how my day-to-day was going, I felt I needed to express my progress and personal victories since my arrival. I decided the best way to do this was through daily affirmations.

An affirmation is a statement that describes a goal in its already completed state. Similar in practice to a mantra, an affirmation is a form of self-talk that stretches your consciousness to a heightened state of being. While a mantra tends to carry an overarching goal and theme, an affirmation can be specific to the day, the intention you need, or the gratitude you feel.

Before embarking on my travels, I thoroughly researched the power of the Law of Attraction and read just about every book linked to it. As a way to cope with my Nonno's passing, I wanted to immerse myself in methods that would transform my thoughts into a more positive state. Not only did I journal and explore what I wanted to achieve, but I also wrote down my travel goals as though they'd been realized. This instantly lifted my mood and put me in control.

Practicing affirmations became a nightly ritual for me, filling me with inspiration and hope. Over the course of the weeks leading up to my trip, I became an expert on the Law of Attraction and corresponding strategies of practicing affirmations.

On that sunny day on the west coast of Thailand, thousands of miles from anyone familiar, I wanted to reaffirm the gratitude beaming from my heart. I walked over to the full-length mirror in my bungalow, stood tall and proud and made eye contact with myself. I knew I was fulfilling my travel dreams and couldn't help but smile. Looking back at my happy reflection created the warmest feeling inside and elevated my mood even further. Smiling at myself in the mirror was the first step in my affirmation practice.

There I stood—smiling at myself like a creep and loving every minute of it. While some may find this awkward, I found it motivational. With that, I took it one level creepier and said affirmations out loud while maintaining eye contact with myself. This became the second phase of my affirmation process.

I affirmed, "I am happy and grateful to be living my dreams." Next, and similar to the mantra I created enroute to the airport, I affirmed, "I am a brave, adventurous and strong person." Finally,

I affirmed what I wanted to attract, "I am open to meeting new friends and encountering unique and fulfilling experiences during my travels."

Reciting these affirmations out loud emitted positive energy into the universe and attracted fulfilling events into my life that would reflect these words. I spoke of the desired outcomes of my travels as though they'd already transpired. And I believed every word. In this third and final phase in the affirmation process, belief was of the utmost importance.

I continued to say affirmations in the mirror throughout my travels. As I reconnected to this positive action, I opened the door to endless possibilities that were already in the process of coming into my life. The momentum of my positive energy allowed me to be open to new adventures and opportunities. As my travel crew and I set out to our next destination, the popular Phi Phi (pronounced Pee-Pee) Islands, I was suspended in the most splendid version of myself.

RECITE DAILY AFFIRMATIONS

A simple exercise of smiling and saying nice things to yourself in a mirror creates such monumental results. Smiling on the outside immediately makes you smile on the inside. It also allows the process of attracting positivity into your life to begin.

I affirmed what I wanted as opposed to what I didn't want. I refused to send a message of "no" out there. If I were to say "I don't ever want to feel sad again about losing my job," the past hurt I once felt would resurface. By using positive language, I could turn it around by saying, "I am grateful for having the freedom to create my own future." Instead, this conjures up feelings of hope and excitement for what's ahead. The universe hears strong, positive messages and will work its magic to make good things happen.

CALL TO ACTION

Allow yourself to have solitude and recite daily affirmations. The three-step process is simple:

Position yourself in front of a mirror, and make eye contact while you smile.

Speak your positive affirmations out loud. It makes your thoughts real and accountable.

Believe the words you're saying with all the truth in your soul, and know it will come to fruition.

LIFE LESSON NINE:
LET GO OF FEAR

*"Expose yourself to your deepest fear; after that, fear has no power,
and the fear of freedom shrinks and vanishes. You are free."*
– Jim Morrison

*E*very now and then, search engines release a list of the most
beautiful beaches to visit in the world. Without any deviation
from the top 10, the Phi Phi Islands are a favourite on the list. This
was where the Leonardo DiCaprio movie, *The Beach*, was filmed.
Naturally, the image of a tanned Leo frolicking along a white sand
beach played in my head as we travelled there.

My travel crew and I first caught glimpse of this paradise on
our ferryboat ride from Phuket. As soon as I saw the white sand
beach and lush tropical trees, tears welled up in my eyes. I was overwhelmed by the island's beauty. I relished in that moment of reflection a minute longer, then gave everyone around me a high-five to
celebrate our arrival.

After settling into my guesthouse, I took an exploratory stroll
around the island. It's only a few miles in circumference, so I grabbed
a delicious fresh coconut from the nearest refreshment stand and set
out. You could not have paid me to stop smiling as I soaked up
everything around me, from the beach bars to the souvenir kiosks to
the long boats lining the shore—I was in my glory!

The island also happened to be a sleepy scuba town where every second shop on the main walking path promoted scuba diving packages. While most tourists are dazzled by this attraction, I tried to avoid eye contact with any of the sales rep from the shops. As you may recall, Ang Urquhart does not like fish and deep water. Actually, it's a bit more dramatic than that. I am absolutely terrified.

In a scuba diving-type situation, it's my understanding that predatory sea creatures lurk in the shadows of the deep water, ready to strike at any moment. I'd always envisioned that once I was submerged in the water, fish would nibble at my feet and violate me. This is a palpable, paralyzing fear of mine.

I continued my stroll around the island, eyes narrowed to the path in front of me, when I heard a familiar Canadian accent. Like a moth to a flame, I followed the recognizable accent and found myself in a riveting conversation with a friendly fellow Canadian, who also happened to be the top-selling scuba rep on the entire western seaboard of Thailand. Damn it all to hell.

While I thought we were simply cultivating a friendship and planning to go for drinks later, somehow I was simultaneously registering for the scuba diving lesson at 7:00 a.m. the next morning. My need to be friends with everyone outweighed my fear of fish and deep water.

The next morning, I arrived at the dock for the scuba lesson. Fear took control of my body, masking the tan on my face. Why, God? Why did I register to do this? I looked out at the choppy water and my heart began to race. This was happening. Along with the other scuba participants, I boarded the boat that took us to our dive spot, and I was introduced to my instructor, a massive German fellow named Dingo. I asked no questions.

After 25 minutes of traveling to our location and 25 minutes of praying for my life, it was time to jump into the water. It may have been my mind playing tricks on me, but the waves seemed extra intense this day. I like to identify myself as a strong swimmer in a pool setting, but as soon as I plunged into the water, I felt paralyzed with the weight of the scuba gear, not to mention my fear, on me. I frantically looked around and saw the faint outline of fish maneuvering through the water. I strategically treaded water to stay away from any threatening sea life. My fear distracted me from thinking clearly, and also from paying attention to the lesson. I hadn't been listening when Dingo explained how to breathe with the air mask and adapt to the pressure changes when lowering into the water. Obviously, when the time came to slip under the water into scuba mode, I wasn't doing it correctly.

I was breathing twice as fast as I should've been, now in full panic mode. And then, of course, I started to cry. I had let fear get the best of me. I was ready to call it quits and tan on the upper deck of our scuba boat for the rest of the day. That was, however, until Travel Ang appeared.

Travel Ang is my self-proclaimed alter ego who is fearless, positive, open-minded and easily adaptable to uncomfortable situations. For the first time during my travels, this bold version of myself emerged from the turquoise blue waters of Thailand. This alter ego is reminiscent of famous images in popular culture, including my hero, Beyoncé, who has a similar persona, named Sasha Fierce.

I didn't want to be crying in the water any more. I wanted to revel in this incredible experience, just as I'd affirmed the day before. Scuba diving in Thailand? That's awesome. I needed to shake off my fear and turn things around. I channelled Beyoncé's alter ego's ferocity and ability to take on anything. By tuning into this self-created character of strength, I let go of all that held me back. Instead of forever contemplating every reason not to do something, fearful of the worst possible outcome, I became fierce and went for it.

I grabbed Dingo's massive hand, kicked my flippers with purpose, and pressurized foot by foot into the magical sea. Once I connected to fearless Travel Ang, I was able to appreciate the magnificence of life under water, including the glorious aquamarine, sea foam green and velvety purple colours that peppered the underwater seascape;

the schools of fish that danced in a formation of pristine choreography; and even the sharks that swam nearby. I appreciated it all.

I left my scuba lesson with a certificate of completion and a new life lesson. With the bar set a little higher for myself, I was ready and eager to tackle the next new adventure my travels would soon present.

LET GO OF FEAR

I remember when someone first told me the acronym for FEAR is False Evidence Appearing Real—I lost my mind. Those four words completely summarize what fear is and what my predicament was in this scuba diving scenario. My imagination created a negative outcome. The feared, negative outcome is only thought, not reality.

Fear creates limiting thoughts and can distance you from actions that could lead to personal growth and positive change. When fear takes over, you become entranced in the feared potential outcome. While the possibility of that outcome (i.e. fish abusing you) may be miniscule, fear relentlessly obscures your capabilities.

With fear befalls the action of escape and avoidance, as fear clashes with your personal status quo. Fear brings forth discomfort, so you retreat and keep away from the actions attributed to that fearful emotion. It can hold you back from experiencing many wonderful things in the world and can even stop you from achieving your dreams. It can distance you becoming the best version of yourself.

You have the capacity to tap into your personal power when you recognize that you're not controlled by your fears. You simply need to let those hindering thoughts go. Recognize your fear as an illusion and you will expand the range of your capabilities.

When you let go of fear, try new things and challenge yourself, you're able to tap into diverse elements of your personality that may be dormant. You build more confidence in your abilities, develop new ways of thinking, new habits, and new opportunities to grow as a person.

CALL TO ACTION

The next time you're faced with fear, assess the factors that may be contributing to it by asking yourself the following:

Is this fear something your mind has created as a defense mechanism?

Is feeling fear a habitual response in certain situations?

Are you faced with something new, which brings you into unknown and fearful territory?

Treat this as an opportunity to challenge yourself. Do something previously unthinkable and step past those barriers of fear. Let go of your self-limiting thoughts and embrace the new emotions and excitement that will undoubtedly arise.

LIFE LESSON TEN: STEP OUT OF YOUR COMFORT ZONE

"Move out of your comfort zone. You can only grow if you are willing to feel awkward and uncomfortable when you try something new."

—Brian Tracy

*O*f there were ever a combination of items that equate to pure hilarity *and* absolute terror for me, it'd be this: Ang Urquhart, camping, and the Phi Phi Islands. I had just conquered my fear of scuba diving with the mysterious fish of the sea and, with newfound confidence, I decided to stretch my fear-vanquishing capabilities even further.

The Phi Phi Islands are comprised of two main islands: Phi Phi Lei and Phi Phi Don, which gained popularity when the smaller island, Lei, was the location for the movie, *The Beach*. The specific beach, Maya Bay, is where most of the movie was filmed and has become a tourist hot spot. I live for anything to do with Hollywood, so if you throw a beach into the mix, well I've reached my happy place. That beach was undoubtedly one of my top places to visit while in Thailand. Since I wanted to experience the beach to its fullest and keep my adventurous Travel Ang persona, I booked an overnight camping trip on Maya Bay.

Time out.

I have NEVER been camping before…

Time in.

Until that point, the most rustic experience I had was staying overnight at a luxury cottage in the Muskokas of Ontario. I also once got lost in a forest during a grade seven class trip. I chose not to reveal this to my camping buddies, the lovely British couple Jackie and John, who I assured I'd be ideal company (though I was crashing their romantic vacation). Although I lacked camping skills, I decided to go into this experience with the attitude I'd adopted throughout my travels: an open mind and loving heart. Jackie, John, and I boarded a cute little tugboat with about 20 other wide-eyed tourists and made our way to our camping destination.

The island of Phi Phi Lei is a nature reserve with no electricity, hotels, restaurants, or anything touristy. The only people who inhabit the Island are bird nest harvesters—Thai people who harvest special nests found only in the Island's limestone caves. The harvesters dedicate their lives to carefully farming the nests until they're at an optimal circumference and girth. After reaching the ideal condition, they're sold to the Chinese.

Amazingly and, in my opinion, almost disturbingly, Phi Phi Lei nests are one of the most expensive avian products consumed by humans. We learned this fun fact on our boat ride to Maya Bay, upon observing the intricate forts located in the coastal caves where the bird-people live. Totally creepy, but extremely cool!

By sunset, all of the day tours that keep the Island bustling had departed, so our group of 20, including our tour guides and the creepy bird people, were the only ones left on the Island.

We were about 30 minutes from reaching our destination, when the sky suddenly darkened, the clouds opened up, and the fattest and most aggressive raindrops I'd ever seen began to pelt down on us. The excitement I'd been feeling about the Island quickly dissolved with the monsoon-like conditions and was replaced with anxiety. Camping was a challenge for me, so adding rain to the scene did not make me a happy camper (pun totally intended).

It wasn't a gentle rain, either. That I could've handled. Instead, within seconds my clothes were so wet that they clung to my body, my hair hung limp around my face, and I was as miserable as I probably looked. It was a warm rainfall, but it chilled me to the bone. I paced back and forth along the bow of the boat, trying to produce some body heat, but the slippery conditions thwarted my efforts.

I decided instead to make use of this time, and introduced myself to the other campers, referring back to Life Lesson Six: Talk to Strangers. Most of them were British, and I could feel my accent resurfacing Engaging in riveting conversation with my new friends distracted me from the rainstorm, and before I knew it, we arrived at Maya Bay. And, as if on some magical cue, it stopped raining! I looked out at the pristine white sand beach with the jungle in the background and my excitement returned.

We arrived on the Island at dusk. By the time Jackie and I decided to locate the toilets, it was pitch dark and we had to light our way with flashlights. After roaming almost half a mile into the jungle, I witnessed one of the most terrifying images of my life: the washroom on Phi Phi Lei. And just as quickly as it had returned, once again, my happiness and excitement dissolved.

I admit, I have public washroom anxiety and so far on this trip, it was rare to find a place that deserved my stamp of approval. Even back at home, I usually had one of my friends run the tap or hand dryer, or sing a song while I used the facilities. I just can't pee under pressure, especially when I'm in a public setting. So there I was, my washroom anxiety and fear of a creepy jungle scene intersecting, where the washrooms likely hadn't been upgraded in over a century.

Jackie and I inched our way up to the tiny and dilapidated shack, where our noses pinched at the foul stench. We peered into the toilet area and as our vision adjusted to the darkness of the night, our eyes fixated on the enormous sand crab residing in the toilet bowl. I wanted to throw up and cry at the same time. I linked arms with Jackie, lurched her away from the toilet, and sprinted with all I had away that dreadful scene.

I immediately wanted to commission a boat to deliver me to a five-star resort at whatever price they were willing to take. Luckily, Jackie identified my level of stress and encouraged me to have a seat on the beach, relax, and enjoy a Singha Beer. After a few minutes of talking through my anxiety, I decided to tough it out (and found a secret area to do my business).

In three short hours, I had experienced a rollercoaster of emotions. But each time I reached a low point, I emerged and kept going.

I kept surprising myself with everything I was able to push past. The discomfort I faced had been conquered, and as a vibrant magenta sun began to set, I felt at peace on Maya Bay. If only I had Leo there to share in the romance of it all. At nightfall, we gathered around the ambient lighting of the rustic Thai lanterns and enjoyed green curry chicken for dinner. During the meal, our small group of strangers became friends.

After dinner, we dared to consume one of Thailand's most famous drinks: a mixed bucket. Served in a large florescent sand pail, the ingredients contain a mickey of alcohol (roughly 12 shots), the Thai version of Red Bull, and soda pop. Drinking just one will get you feeling good and, with that, the level of fun escalated exponentially.

Thankfully someone had a good mind to pack his guitar, so by the bonfire light, we took part in a sing-along under the starry sky. We created our own fantastic version of *The Beach*, but the difference was that our experience brought us to a special place full of appreciation and bonding.

As the night wore on, my accent grew thicker from bonding with the British folk I'd dubbed my Maya Bay mates. As some of my new friends retired to bed, a few of us decided to camp away from the rest of the group where we could sleep on the beach. With the sound of waves crashing only a few feet away from me, I fell asleep underneath the stars—something I never could've imagined I'd do.

To wake up on Maya Bay was like the continuation of a wonderful dream in which I'm standing there wide-eyed gazing out across the turquoise water and periwinkle blue sky. Alone on the beach, I celebrated a personal victory in pushing through my comfort zone and surviving my first night camping... in, of all places, Thailand.

Our tugboat arrived shortly after sunrise to take us back to Phi Phi Don, bringing our camping expedition on Maya Bay to an end. As we sailed away, I took a moment of solitude and gazed back at the idyllic scenery that was increasingly becoming more distant, soon to be a memory. What would always remain was the strength I garnered in stretching past my perceived limitations. As I ventured on, this strength would only come to grow more powerful.

STEP OUT OF YOUR COMFORT ZONE

On the Island, I identified that I needed to break through the personal limitations and boundaries I had created for myself, which in this case were camping and herding off mysterious animals of the night. Did I want to cry or shake in fear on Maya Bay and cut myself off from people and nature around me? Or, did I want to embrace my surroundings and have a unique once-in-a-lifetime experience? Definitely the latter. I encouraged myself to change my mindset from self-doubt to a new place of receptiveness.

A comfort zone is a behavioural space that's secure, expected, and minimizes risk and stress. It's easy to stay in these familiar zones because it provides security and evenness. When you want to dig deeper and maximize your performance, however, you need to veer from the familiar. More than likely, your deepest dreams lie outside of your comfort zone.

Can you remember a time when you surpassed fear and stepped outside of your comfort zone? How did you feel afterwards? Chances are, you felt sensational. Magic happens when you challenge yourself and increase your confidence by doing things that you normally wouldn't do.

We fear the unfamiliar and often the associated outcomes. Those scary feelings stir up important emotions that help us tap into what we really want. Chances are, when you stay suspended in your comfort zones, there isn't much fluctuation in goal-setting or incentive to strive toward your dreams. This life lesson encourages you to push past those limitations and step into the unknown.

Everyone's comfort zone is different—so what may increase your range of capabilities may paralyze someone else. The important thing is that you take action forward because every small step offers momentum.

The possibilities are endless when you push past the limitations of your comfort zone. You trust yourself more, which enables you to take risks in a controlled fashion, and gain more ambition. Your mental productivity and performance can now peak as you habitually push yourself to the next awesome level.

CALL TO ACTION

Do everyday things a little differently. This brings freshness to your thinking, allowing creativity and inspiration to cultivate.

Start off by simply waking up 15 minutes earlier than usual or try a new restaurant for lunch. Gradually adopt the idea of learning a new skill, instrument, or language, and even embracing travel.

Do something that shakes up your routine and brings you into new, exciting territory.

LIFE LESSON ELEVEN: FIND YOUR ATTITUDE OF GRATITUDE

"As we express our gratitude, we must never forget that the highest appreciation is not to utter words, but to live by them."
– John F. Kennedy

*O*f you asked me to choose one word to describe my first week and a half in Thailand, it would be: luxurious. Every day, my travel crew and I indulged in $5 massages on the beach, followed by cocktails served in pineapples or coconuts. We completed our days with fabulous seaside dinners, sampling Thailand's most exotic curries and spices. I was spoiling myself to the excess.

Even though I was enjoying myself, I had a pang of unsettlement—a pain in the pit of my stomach from unresolved sadness. And more than anything, I missed my Nonno. I knew I needed to take care of this feeling.

One of my Maya Bay mates had recommended the Wat Than Sua, also known as the Tiger Temple, as a must-see place to find peace. With that suggestion in mind, I commissioned a taxi driver to take me to the remote area of Krabi where I could follow my spiritual aspirations.

The Tiger Temple is a pilgrimage point for Buddhist monks, located on a mountaintop overlooking Krabi, a lush tropical town on the west coast of Thailand. The town boasts the picturesque Railay Beach, a stretch of powder white sand sheltered by towering limestone cliffs. Longboats lined the beach, with hints of authentic Thai culture cascading into the seascape. Simply viewing the scene gave me goose bumps.

To actually reach the temple, I had to first endure a climb of 1,236 steps up through the jungle. In addition to this daunting hike, there was one unique warning posted at the base of the mountain that read, "Beware of the rogue monkeys that inhabit the jungle as they have a habit of stealing." As I organized my belongings for my journey, I saw monkeys lurking in the trees and sizing me up. I'm also pretty sure they were laughing at me. In that moment I regretted packing so many bananas for energy. Luckily, my backpack was like Fort Knox, so any attempts by the monkeys to pick-pocket me were thwarted.

Leaving the threat of monkeys behind, I began my climb, feeling confident in my ability to crush the stairs in double time since I'd been running along the beaches all week. This was wildly presumptuous of me. Not only were the steps narrow, but each one was set higher and further away than the last, so one step was like walking up two. That, combined with the heat and extreme humidity, contributed to an agonizing trek up the mountain. After 40 minutes of working my glutes like they'd never been worked before, I finally reached the stunning hilltop temple.

Sometimes, I feel my life and its events work as though they're a scene from a movie. The moment I reached the top of the Tiger Temple, completely exhausted from the uphill journey (but exhilarated too), light rain began to fall. I looked around and was taken aback by the golden Buddha statues lining the temple, glistening from the rain. Was I really there?

Once I realized I was the only one up there, the solitutde allowed me to transcend from the physical strain my body was feeling to a state of tranquility. I knew this moment was an important, peaceful one. I let go of the feeling of sadness lingering over me. With that release, I fell to tears of joy and gratitude, and somehow I knew my Nonno's spirit was there with me.

Much like the hurdle of dealing with my Nonno's death, I struggled with the challenging journey to the top of the temple. Although painful at times, I kept moving forward. As I reached the top of the mountain of the Tiger Temple, I paused and reflected on both my journey to live without my Nonno and my journey up the mountain. In both scenarios, I had to confront the challenge and take steps (both literally and figuratively) to overcome it. By doing this, I welcomed clarity of mind. I welcomed peace.

I sat in the perfect spot overlooking the magnificent scenery and took a few moments of stillness and further reflection on my life. I was overwhelmed with gratitude and I could sense my soul beginning to heal. The negative energy and sadness had lifted. I felt lighter.

I'd kept a journal since the beginning of my travels, and in that moment I felt compelled to write special prayers of light and love for not only my Nonno in heaven, but also the wonderful people in my life.

At the top of a fresh page in my journal, I wrote, **I am so happy and grateful for**…, and listed those closest to me in my life. Fueled by thankfulness, I continued, listing my family, friends, teachers, and some material items I was fortunate enough to have. I was in Thailand on the top of a mountain and writing. This was my life, and boy, was I ever grateful!

Sure, the previous few months had been filled with turmoil and sadness, but instead of focusing on those difficult moments, I focused on all the amazing things in my life. My emotional and spiritual state, as I sat on that mountaintop perched above the beaches of Thailand, was of pure appreciation for what had been and what was to come. Suspended in this attitude of gratitude, I was now receptive to even more things to come into my life that I could be grateful for. Gratitude leads to the magical position of abundance, so why not focus on the good and be grateful?

A number of modern day self-help books suggest the concept of making a gratitude journal. On top of the Tiger Temple, I created mine. I took quiet time to sit and reflect on the people in my life and experiences I've had, which brought me to a heightened state of appreciation. It brought me to love. Feeling grateful and sending out positive intentions to the universe enlightened me to find another life lesson and best version of myself.

I'm not certain I could have previously given an example of when I felt at peace. After the experience at the Tiger Temple, I knew I'd reached an enriched part of my personal growth that would positively affect me moving forward. I now have a point of reference for experiencing this personal harmony, a place I choose to revisit through the simple yet beautiful life lesson of gratitude.

FIND YOUR ATTITUDE OF GRATITUDE

By adopting an attitude of gratitude, you change the way you look at the world. You can view your life from an appreciative and loving stance, embracing the beauty encircling you. Practicing gratitude simply makes you happier, more peaceful, and connects you to living your best life.

When you focus on all of the wonderful things in your life, your entire energy shifts to a more positive place. You can feel satisfied and appreciative for the abundance that is already present, instead of focusing on anything perceived to be lacking.

CALL TO ACTION

Take time to meditate and reflect on what you're thankful for by creating your own gratitude journal. Begin with the abundance that already surrounds you.

Select a journal that reflects your style. (Mine had bright colours and whimsical fun shapes.)

Write the words, I am so happy and grateful for...

List people (friends, family, teachers, colleagues, your friendly neighbour, etc.).

List experiences (that trip to Florida, that birthday party, that awesome movie you just watched).

List possessions (house, car, patio set, backpack).

Make your journal easily accessible so you are able to add to it whenever the moment strikes you. A list is something you may only look at once, where a journal is something to which you can continually add.

Let there be no limitations. Feel your energy soar with gratitude and joy.

LIFE LESSON TWELVE:
LOSE YOURSELF IN MUSIC

"I think music in itself is healing. It's an explosive expression of humanity. It's something we are all touched by. No matter what culture we're from, everyone loves music."
— Billy Joel

My experience at the Tiger Temple was the perfect way to complete the first phase of my travels. I parted ways with my original travel crew, Jackie, John, and Rob. I took a moment to express gratitude for the brief, yet quality friendships that positively affected my first few weeks on the other side of the world.

Once again, I was on my own and now ready to conquer the eastern islands of Thailand.

I walked to the bus terminal and booked a one-way ticket to Koh Samui, an island off the east coast of Thailand, that came highly recommended by a number of my Maya Bay mates as an essential stop.

However, there was one massive catch. To get there, I would have to endure a six-hour bus ride from one coast to the other. Then, take a ferry ride, another bus ride, and a taxi ride to my new location (yet to be determined at that point) on the Island. It was quite the travel commitment, but I was eager to explore and venture into the unknown.

Traveling by bus in Thailand isn't the most luxurious mode of travel. The seats seemed to be sized for children, not a grown woman like myself who teeters just under six ft. tall. The air conditioner on the bus, which functioned more like a space heater and only worked sporadically, hit me with warm and even warmer air—never cool.

And as if I weren't uncomfortable enough, a tiny Swedish boy sat next to me, slipping in and out of consciousness, while resting his sweaty head on my shoulder. Why do people keep doing this to me? I don't know if it's my comfortable shoulder or just a traveller thing to do. Maybe my life lesson of talking to strangers was translating into cuddling with strangers. Whatever it was, I wasn't on board.

A typical response to an annoying situation like this one might be to drown in complaints and negativity. Truth be told, it sucked. But given my limited funds, the bus was my only option. So, I was stuck like this for *hours*. I bordered on falling into the downward complaint spiral, but caught myself and shifted gears. The only thing I could do to mentally escape was listen to music and daydream.

Insert new line item to my gratitude journal: I am very grateful for iPods.

Music has been shown to affect the autonomic nervous system—the part responsible for controlling blood pressure, heartbeat, and brain function. Listening to music creates a dynamic relationship with our physiological, emotional, and cognitive health. Slow rhythms of music, for example, provide an almost sedative tone. This can relax the body, both physically and mentally, calming a cluttered mind. High energy and fast tempo music, on the other hand, serves to boost our mood, motivate us, and contribute to releasing endorphins—the natural "feel good" hormones that bring us happiness. We listen to certain upbeat music, and we become happy. Simply put, our favourite songs lift our spirits.

For me, songs transform into personal soundtracks. Certain songs become engrained in my makeup, providing me with solace and comfort. In other scenarios, music allows me to connect with my creativity and inspiration. I tend to attach music to a time, place, or a particular memory, so when I hear certain songs, I time-travel back to that moment.

My absolute favourite thing to do is choreograph dances in my head or pretend I'm part of a music video, in which I'm the star. I'm able to lose myself in the song and escape whatever stress or sadness I'm facing (like a wildly uncomfortable bus ride).

As I settled into the second hour of the bus ride, I shifted from my "Upbeat Travel Tunes" playlist to my "Chill Acoustic Jams" playlist. I rested my head against the window, gazing out at the scenery unfolding before me. With the gentle strumming of a guitar to calm my mind, I momentarily forgot I was cradling the head of a tiny Swedish boy to my left. My annoyance had dissipated and was replaced by a relaxed vibe. All it took was the right song.

LOSE YOURSELF IN MUSIC

By losing yourself in music, you transcend sender-receiver barriers. You become the artist and the lyrics become your story. You find common threads with shared emotions and experiences. The message transmitted through the song allows you to connect to the music, like a list of memories. I was so fortunate to call on these warm and comfortable memories while riding on a hot, stinky and bouncy bus. This was escapism at its finest!

CALL TO ACTION

Music is a subjective art form to which different people respond in different ways. If you're feeling the not-so-best version of yourself, try the following:

Find a space where you can freely listen to music. This can be anywhere from the solitude of your bedroom to sitting outside on your back porch to going to your favourite spot at the park. Throw on your favourite music and become lost in the sounds. Whether it is Bob Marley, Madonna, Beyoncé, or Metallica, choose music that evokes happiness within you.

Let the music move you and filter through your body. Different moods call for different music, so whatever your mood add the element of music that fits best and see how it can change the energy entirely.

You can also do the following:

Make playlists according to your mood, time of the year, or vibe (i.e. Happy Summer Jams, Weekend Vibe, Mellow Jazz Tunes, etc.)

Pick out your own customized playlist. You can use Songza and the work is already done!

Crank up the tunes and sing your face off!

Notice how instantly your tone changes and your spirit elevates!

LIFE LESSON THIRTEEN:
EAT MINDFULLY

"Our bodies are our gardens—our wills are our gardeners"
—William Shakespeare

After serenading my Swedish bus companion for a few hours with my favourite Bob Marley tunes in a Jamaican accent that sounded almost too good, I emerged from the bus and headed towards the pier to continue my travels.

On the ferry ride to the Island of Koh Samui, I discussed possible guesthouses with the tour operator on board. My next destination was a little village named Lamai. He showed me a picture of a beautiful resort with lush gardens and private rustic bungalows overlooking the ocean. Rustic being the operative word.

Here's a bonus mini life lesson within this chapter, which I stress with the utmost of importance: ALWAYS physically view a guesthouse before booking and paying for it.

By the time I arrived at the accommodations, which I had prepaid for en route (rookie mistake), it was nighttime and pouring rain. The shadows seemed to be extra dark and ominous, and there was an eerie energy in the air. Perhaps the weather attributed to my overall impression of the place, but for the first time in Thailand, I didn't feel safe.

My experience in Lamai was marked by revolving accommodations. I changed guesthouses three times in three days, unable to fall into a comfortable groove. I was unsettled. My energy was low and bordering on negative. Identifying my personal unrest, I knew I had to shift to a positive place. Back in Canada, when I felt down or anxious, I would attend a yoga class to make me feel better.

One of my Maya Bay mates had mentioned a yoga and wellness centre where she'd been on Koh Samui. When something peaked my interest during my travels, I wrote it in my journal. I referred back to my notes, and realized the wellness centre, named Spa Samui, was only a short distance away. I grabbed my backpack, a quick latte and croissant, hopped into a taxi, and excitedly made my way there for a yoga class.

I arrived a few minutes later to a quaint and charming beach resort set amidst palm trees along the shoreline. This setting, paired with the spa-like atmosphere, instantly put me back on track. I was greeted by a lovely Thai girl, Jennifer, who briefed me on the yoga and meditation elements to the centre. She continued on about Spa Samui's offerings and described the main component of the wellness centre: fasting programs.

After I discussed all the possible outcomes with Jennifer, I concluded that fate had led me to Spa Samui and I promptly signed up for the four-day fast. This perfectly aligned with my Dramatically Zen way of being. It was also something I had been interested in doing ever since I learned that Beyoncé had done something similar to prepare for her role in the movie, *Dreamgirls*. It was a very celeb thing to do, so I was intrigued. Without the distractions and temptations of home (like going out for drinks, hanging out at Starbucks enjoying sugary lattes, or grabbing dinner with friends), Thailand would be the perfect location for this endeavor.

I was given my fasting program package containing the agenda of what my next four days would entail. I'd already broken fasting rule number one: prepare your body. I should've been consuming only raw fruits and vegetables for two days before the program. The buttery croissant and caramel latte I had in the taxi to Spa Samui were a major no-no. As I read through the strict program, I questioned what I'd gotten myself into. I'd gone to Spa Samui to partake in yoga classes, not to participate in an intense fast. What was I thinking? How could I deny myself all the scrumptious Thai food and fresh fruits and Singha beers? How could I refuse the cornucopia of deliciousness surrounding me everywhere I went? I travelled thousands and thousands of miles only to NOT eat? But, I'd already registered and given them my credit card information, so there was no turning back.

A typical fasting day was divided into hour and a half blocks and looked something like this:

7:00 a.m.   Wake up. Drink psyllium husk mixed with freshly squeezed pineapple juice.

8:30 a.m.   Take a vitamin. (What it was was indeed a mystery, but I trusted the staff of the Spa Samui)

10:00 a.m.   Drink vegetable broth (Water where vegetables are steamed; no salt and no flavour).

11:30 a.m.   Take another mystery vitamin.

1:00 p.m.   Drink signature Liver Flush Drink, a mix of fresh orange and lime juice, olive oil, garlic and cayenne pepper. (Author's note: Again, this reminded me of something I'd heard Beyoncé consumed in preparation for her role in *Dreamgirls*. I channelled my inner Beyoncé each time I drank this concoction.)

2:30 p.m.   Take the last mystery vitamin for the day.

4:00 p.m.   Drink freshly made carrot juice, followed by the Colema Board (Basically, a colon-cleanse. I've never been so scared in my life.)

5:30 p.m.   Gulp down more vegetable broth, which by this
             point had grown on me tremendously.

7:00 p.m.   Drink coconut water from a young coconut—the
             best natural source to replenish your electrolytes.

A dozen or so other patrons were taking part in the same
program, so I was able to plan my days alongside my fasting friends
and we encouraged each other. On day one of my fast, I felt motivated, powerful, and happy.

On day two, however, that happiness mutated into psychosis.
The sugar and carbohydrates that usually framed my days were
replaced by watered down vegetable boringness and I could feel
myself getting restless, cranky, and above everything else, hungry.
I was ready to throw in the towel and scarf down a plate of $0.80
pad thai as fast as humanly possible. But no—I was determined.
So, when my fasting friend (a Scottish woman named Lesley), suggested distracting ourselves by getting a Thai massage, I immediately agreed.

We made our way to the recommended massage parlour down
the street, where a lovely Thai woman, who stood approximately
four ft. tall, greeted us. If there's anything I learned in that hour and
a half, it's not to judge a person's abilities by their size. The teeny
Thai woman was, in fact, freakishly strong. As she rolled me up like
a ball and folded me into a human pretzel, I wasn't sure whether to
laugh or cry! This torture, which I believe included such Western
techniques as roundhouse kicking and steamrolling, lasted an
agonizing hour and twenty minutes. I left the massage parlour in
intense pain and feeling somewhat violated, but at least my mind
was no longer fixated on hunger.

I eventually fell into the groove of the fast, and by day three it
became purely mental instead of physical. I felt an unprecedented
control and presence in my body.

The fast was a catalyst for changing the way I approach food. I now have an appreciation for food's nutritional content and how it serves to fuel and nourish my body. The experience has had a profound impact on when, how much, and of what quality I eat. The most important take-away from the fasting experience was how to adopt a new mindfulness to my eating process.

Deep down, we know what we should and shouldn't eat, but we distance ourselves from eating healthy because unhealthy foods taste better, are usually cheaper, or easier to prepare. While it provides immediate gratification to have that cheesy plate of nachos (a personal fave), hoagie, or plate of fries, whenever I indulge that way, I suffer from food remorse. This is followed by feelings of depression and discouragement.

I feel much better about my choices and my self-esteem when I eat properly (i.e. factoring fruits and vegetables into every meal). When you think about it, how delicious and satisfying is it to have a bite out of a fresh piece of fruit or a crisp vegetable? Why not eat more like this and continue to feel great?

A few days into the fast, I felt back on track. Those initial feelings of unsettlement I had when I arrived were replaced by feelings of empowerment.

EAT MINDFULLY

I garnered this simple life lesson from my fasting experience: eat mindfully. Choose a balanced diet, eat locally, eat vegetables, eat nutrients, drink plenty of water, and be aware of the immediate response with not only your energy, but with your level of happiness.

It's empowering to know that you're bigger than your habits and cravings. You determine your well-being through what you put in your body. By selecting proper foods to eat, you nourish and energize yourself. You feel alive and excited, not sluggish and depressed.

By eating mindfully, you liberate yourself to take charge of how you fuel your body and live your life.

CALL TO ACTION

A full-blown fast in Thailand may not be the most accessible first step, but you can start by deciding to mindfully select your meals. Take control of your food choices and your body. You'll gain a presence in your body and in turn will have positive feelings about yourself.

Try a few of the following suggestions today to feel empowered to eat mindfully:

Come up with a meal plan for the week. This way, you set yourself up for success and bring that important mindfulness to your meals.

Find a healthier alternative to sugary or salty snacks, such as hummus and veggies, or even organic tortilla chips and salsa.

Research some fun and healthy recipes online, then carve out a night to try them!

Try a fast or cleanse. Check out local health stores, and try a sugar or gluten cleanse. It can simply start with a three-day cleanse.

Set realistic goals!

LIFE LESSON FOURTEEN: BRING YOGA INTO YOUR LIFE

"Peace. It does not mean to be in a place where there is no noise,
trouble or hard work. It means to be in the midst of those things
and still be calm in your heart."
—Unknown

On the third day of my fast, I decided to pursue what originally brought me to Spa Samui: a yoga class. My soul had been craving yoga, but I'd become distracted by the mechanics of the fast. Now that I was into the groove, I figured it was a good time to try out a class. Sure, I was a little weak, but I had a unique sense of clarity and presence in my mind and body. I was ready.

Many years ago, a group of spiritual men in ancient India created a series of postures to prepare the body for hours in meditation, but over time, the practice evolved into a physical challenge to connect the mind, body, and spirit—a way to be present and find inner peace. This is how yoga as we know it came to be.

Connecting to that present mind is the biggest challenge for me, as my mind tends to be filled with clutter, lists of things to do, and worries. But at Spa Samui, I felt grounded. I felt peaceful. Yoga was a perfect way to enhance these feelings.

I made my way to a mid-morning class. The "yoga sala" (a sophisticated and exotic way to say yoga space), was an elevated stage of ebony wood surrounded by tropical flowers and exquisite mini-palm trees. It was open-aired and looked over the A-frame Thai huts surrounding the infinity pool along the beach. The yoga instructor, Anna, radiated light and love. As soon as I stepped into the yoga sala and onto my mat, I tingled with excitement. This was exactly what I needed!

Vinyasa is my favourite type of yoga style because it resembles a beautiful dance through the action of connecting sun salutations. Conveniently, Anna used this style of yoga during my first practice. We took approximately eight minutes at the beginning of the class to become centered and calm. The centering exercise, consisting of simple pranayama (breath work), drew my attention away from any lingering thoughts and allowed me to focus on my inhalation and exhalation.

Then it really got good. We began our flow in the initial stoic standing posture of tadasana (mountain pose in Sanskrit, the language of yoga). I inhaled deeply and joyously reached my arms up to the sky. From here, we engaged in a series of sun salutation A's and B's, gradually progressing in speed. I felt powerful transitioning from posture to posture, occasionally taking pause in downward facing dog. I was feeling the flow.

After an hour of this blissful Vinyasa class, I slowed my mind and body as I prepared myself for savasana (Sanskrit for corpse pose). This death-like asana (posture) at the end of practice allows you to relax, restore, and regenerate. Reclining along my mat, I extended my legs, a little wider than hip distance apart, while lengthening my arms alongside my body, palms up. I tucked my shoulder blades underneath my back, tilted my chin in towards my chest, parted my teeth and closed my eyes. I inhaled deeply through my nose and let out a long exaggerated sigh, releasing any other tension I was holding onto. I let the warmth of the tropical climate envelop me like a big beautiful hug and allowed a peacefulness to take over. My body was smiling from the inside out. With mindful consideration of my breath, I harmoniously allowed myself to delve deeper into this final relaxation pose.

Anna directed the class to bring awareness back into our bodies, gently moving our fingers and toes, then rolling out our wrists and ankles. She instructed us to reach our arms up for a full body stretch, as though we were waking up for the first time. I rolled over to one side, then pushed myself up to a seated position, facing Anna. She bowed and very gently said, "Namaste," which means "the light within me honours the light within you." We all bowed and said "Namaste" in unison. A smile emerged on my face, and I felt an all-encompassing feeling of joy. This is what I like to call yoga magic. One hundred percent of the time, I leave a yoga class feeling good. A magical sense of joy reveals itself after waking from the final relaxation pose of savasana.

Yoga is something I practice to consistently find my peace and my happiness. It allows me to become aware of my fundamental goodness as well as the goodness of others. Yoga offers the assurance that through sincere, thoughtful, and consistent practice, anyone can be happy, peaceful, and free. This feeling is sustained long after stepping off the mat and resonates through the day-to-day. A little bit of mental and physical application, and the mind, body, and soul connect, leaving you with a magical feeling.

Each day at Spa Samui, I applied this life lesson and knew I was connecting to the best version of myself. The unsettling feeling I had when I arrived at Spa Samui was gone, and my energy was transformed to a positive state.

BRING YOGA INTO YOUR LIFE

Yoga encourages you to honour your body and practice according to your abilities. In bringing awareness to your body, you can stretch beyond your perceived limitations by stepping out of your comfort zone. It isn't a competition. It's a personal challenge to apply your physical capabilities to personal practice. Let go of your ego and your self-criticism and allow yourself to be present and happy in the space you're in. This mindset allows you to live fearlessly, thus opening up new experiences and possibilities.

Yoga may be a regular part of your routine, or it may be a foreign concept to you. This life lesson encourages you to get yourself on a mat, breathe slowly and mindfully, and be present in the moment. You don't have to be a circus-like contortionist with the ability to manipulate your body into a human pretzel. Wherever you are in your level of practice is perfect.

CALL TO ACTION

It's simple.

Do yoga!

Yoga is accessible for any level. The number of yoga studios that have opened in the last few years is a testament to the worth of this practice.

Check out your local yoga studio and try different styles of yoga to see what meshes with your needs. It could be a gentle hatha class or a rigorous hot Vinyasa class.

If going to a class is too intimidating, you can search YouTube for, "yoga for beginners;" "yoga for your hips;" or "yoga for relaxation." The options are endless!

Give it a try and feel that undeniable yoga magic!

LIFE LESSON FIFTEEN: MEDITATE

"We cannot see our reflection in running water. It is only in still water that we can see."

–Zen quote

𝓘'm undoubtedly Dramatically Zen. I search for experiences that bring me to a place of peace and enlightenment, yet the path I follow is never smooth. More times than not, it is done in the most dramatic of ways.

One universally accepted method of achieving a state of Zen is through meditation. It's a technique to quiet the mind, where you bring yourself to stillness within your soul. This translates to peacefulness in your day-to-day actions.

Meditation is something I've struggled with over the years. It didn't come easy, so I avoided the practice altogether. While in Thailand though, I felt meditation was a perfect complement to my yoga commitment.

I knew the benefits of meditation: it creates a clear mind; brings about a knowledge of self; aids in concentration; provides emotional stability; helps to release stress; and has a multitude of healing benefits for the body. I knew it was a beneficial practice. So why did I always resist anything that remotely resembled meditation?

At Spa Samui, where I had made a personal contract to cleanse my mind, body, and soul, I decided to give meditation another chance and signed up for the group meditation class held every day at 7:30 a.m.

When I arrived at the class that first morning, eight others were already seated comfortably in the meditation circle. I joined the group and perched myself on a small pillow, relishing in the sounds of the sea in the background. The morning breeze was warm and comfortable, and I already felt I'd transcended into the meditation zone before the class started. I winked at the person across from me and gave the thumbs up to the person on my left, sending out positive and supportive energy to let them know I was on the same page Zen-wise.

Our meditation leader floated into the room and greeted us warmly, clearly embodying the peaceful aura of one perpetually in a meditative state. I liked him immediately. That was, until he informed us that for the next hour we would be seated in silence, eyes closed, to initiate meditation.

Wait. One hour? I'd been thinking a twenty-minute session tops, which had already made me uncomfortable. One hour seemed like the most daunting task imaginable. My self-sabotage started at that precise moment.

As the meditation practice began, my breathing grew frantic, which only made me more anxious. The elements surrounding suddenly disagreed with me. My face was itchy, the temperature was too hot, and I could hear bees buzzing around me. (Ang Urquhart does not like bees.) The initial peaceful atmosphere dissipated.

I tried desperately not to psych myself out, but it was too late. I'd already defeated myself at the prospect of a full hour of meditation, and within two minutes I was in panic mode. Instead of concentrating on a quiet mind and my breathing, I focused on all the annoyances— and seriously, were there really fifty-eight minutes left? I figured this is what it must feel like when you go crazy. I opened my eyes, looked around me, and became even more annoyed and borderline angry. Everyone in the circle was calm and Zen, and there I was having a slight panic attack.

Seeing my fellow meditation friends in their peaceful state made me want to achieve my own peace. I gave my head a shake and convinced myself to start fresh. I took a couple of deep breaths and started over. This process of panic and peace continued for the next half-hour.

After my initial anxiety settled down, I became calm. I felt a little spark of joy creep up within me and a smile formed on my face. All those self-sabotaging thoughts of, *I can't meditate,* were released and my mind became clear. I continued to breathe and slow my heart rate. For the final minutes of the practice, I felt relaxed. I was at peace.

While I knew a 60-minute meditation session was too much for me, practicing meditation was too good not to try again. All I needed to do was reassess the situation and fine-tune the experience according to what would work for me. Instead of joining class the next morning, I went to the beach and sat for five minutes of meditation. Taking that time to become present with my mind and to create stillness in my body left me feeling great for the entire day.

MEDITATE

When you first sit down to meditate, you notice how cluttered your mind can be. Like anything of value, meditation takes practice and a touch of determination. To get started with your own meditation practice, focus on your breathing. Direct your thoughts to your inhalation and exhalation, and draw out your breath longer and longer as you go on. This will point your concentration in one way and block out negative thoughts that serve no purpose.

If you find that your mind is playing games and self-sabotaging, you can incorporate a mantra into the meditation practice. Choose a powerful set of words to chant and focus on, and repeat them over and over in your head until you feel at peace.

It's important to note that every meditation isn't going to be the same. Some days it'll come naturally and you will be able to sit in stillness for lengthy amounts of time. Other days, you may easily succumb to frustration. Be kind to yourself and know that meditation takes time and practice.

Once you get into the meditative zone, this stillness will resonate in your soul and you'll go through your day with presence and awareness. You will be a happier person. By attaining control of your thoughts and infusing them with goodness, you can move forward with optimism in your life.

CALL TO ACTION

Find a quiet spot in your home or in nature with an atmosphere that lends itself to peace.

Sit, breathe, empty your thoughts and be at one with your mind for a few minutes.

OR

Attend a group meditation class at your local yoga studio and experience group energy. This is a completely different experience that may or may not work, but it never hurts to try.

Purchase (or borrow from the library!) a CD on meditation. You can even download guided meditation classes from iTunes. The theme could be anything from calming to attracting abundance to healing.

The resources available for meditation are endless.

LIFE LESSON SIXTEEN:
MAKE WISHES

"Whatever the mind can conceive and believe, it can achieve."
–Napoleon Hill

While at Spa Samui, it happened to be the King of Thailand's birthday (which is a big deal because he apparently is the best guy). To celebrate this special occasion, people gathered along the beaches to light off fireworks and send whimsical lanterns into the sky. Back at home, the purchase of fireworks typically entails my cousins shooting off Roman candles at each other and pissing off the girls. This was quite a different experience.

I'd noticed these lanterns a few weeks earlier while I was in Koh Phi Phi, but didn't grasp their purpose until now. When you light the lantern, which basically looks like a mini hot air balloon, you make a wish. You send it off into the night sky, keeping the intention of your wish while watching the lantern. When you can no longer see it, your wish has been released into the universe to be answered. Simply magical.

I knew immediately that I needed to participate in this beautiful experience!

Over the course of my few days at Spa Samui, I formed strong bonds with the other guests participating in the fasting program. We were all going through similar highs and lows of completing the fast and we offered support and encouragement to one another to push past the lulls. After dinner (also known as coconut water) on the evening of the King's birthday, I suggested we locate the lanterns to celebrate the special occasion. Seven of us wanted to participate, so we purchased one extra-large sized lantern (which stood about three ft. tall) to share our wish-making venture.

We walked down to the beach and observed the enchanting nightscape that unfolded before us. Dozens of Thai lanterns were perfectly scattered across the night sky. They danced above us in a mesmerizing pattern that enhanced the fireworks erupting up and down the beach. As I gazed out, I had to pinch myself because it felt like I was part of a fantastical dream.

Suspended in the mystical atmosphere, my Spa Samui friends and I prepared our lantern to take flight into the night sky. Before lighting it, we each took a moment to set an intention—a wish to be released into the universe. I closed my eyes and visualized what I wanted to achieve from my travels: to feel healed and happy; to inspire others; and to write a book. I felt an unparalleled sensation of hope and complete confidence the universe would work its magic.

We all took one deep breath, lit the lantern, and on the count of three, sent it up into the night sky. We watched the lantern float slowly across the seascape and fade away into darkness.

Making wishes on the beach was the perfect way to end my time in Koh Samui. It was one of the most special and mystical moments I had experienced in my life where I felt complete connectedness to the magical energy in the universe. I look back now at that incredible night and smile with gratitude knowing that my wishes have already come true.

MAKE WISHES

A wish isn't bound by logic, but directs the imagination to a higher and happier way of thinking. Emitting energy and inspired thought out into the universe can do no harm and results in positive feelings.

The birth of a dream lies in the process of tapping into your emotional guidance system and seeing where, without any restrictions, your heart directs you to go. A wish is your innermost desire that can guide you in following through with your dream. Making wishes elicits feelings of happiness through hope and optimism.

After the passing of my Nonno, I took the much-required time to contemplate what made me happy. Within the sadness, I was inspired to view the opposite emotion (positivity) and I journaled about what I wanted out of life. I took time to focus on what inspired me and would make me happy. I came up with a list of wishes, dreams, and goals, which motivated me each time I reviewed the list.

A goal serves to direct our day-to-day actions, whereas a wish takes place a step earlier by contributing to a positive frame of mind to cultivate those goals. This life lesson brings us back to a place of child-like hope and wonderment and the belief that wishes do come true. At what age did we become so jaded and stop believing in the magic of wishes and dreams?

The objective in this life lesson is to strip away the negative conditioning that removes you from the path of achieving your dreams. Limiting your scope enables you to settle, but making wishes and believing in dreams brings you hope. It elevates your spirit to a higher level of thinking.

CALL TO ACTION

What is it you really want in your life? What would be your wish or dream come true? Why not believe that someday your wish can be realized? I suggest starting here:

Make a wish any possible chance you can. Relish any opportunity that presents itself (i.e. at 11:11; while catching feathers; or blowing candles out on your birthday cake).

Take time to establish thoughtful and inspiring wishes. Hold on to each wish or dream in your mind.

Imagine yourself attaining the wish and feel the emotions you would experience once you've attained it. In moving forward with your dream, these emotions should contain only positive elements.

Feel happy when thinking about your dreams and trust that they absolutely can come true.

LIFE LESSON SEVENTEEN: BE PLAYFUL

"We don't stop playing because we grow old; we grow old because we stop playing."
—George Bernard Shaw

The morning after my magical wish-making experience on the beach, my time at Spa Samui was complete. With a heavy heart, I said good-bye to my fasting friends. I left my Zen-like health retreat with another handful of inspiring life lessons as I set out to my next destination: Koh Phangnan.

The name Koh Phangnan derives from the root of the word "gnan," meaning sandbar, referring to the multitude of sandbars offshore surrounding the Island. More than half of the Island is rainforest and designated as a national park. All the action on Koh Phangnan takes place on the coastline, with thriving beach bars, restaurants, and most importantly, the popular beach Haad Rin, which hosts the world-famous "full moon party" that takes place during, you guessed it, the full moon.

It's believed that people act a little crazy during the full moon. Our body composition is about 60 percent water, so if the moon can affect the ocean tides, surely it must have some consequence on human behaviour. The word "lunatic," essentially meaning crazy, comes from the root word "luna," meaning moon. Perhaps people just favour information that feeds the theory, pointing out odd behaviour during the full moon, whereas any other time of the month it would be a quiet observation. The party in Thailand plays up the crazy factor, thus setting the scene for one of the most massive and outrageous beach parties in the world.

My upcoming experiences on the tiny Island would be a far cry from the days of serenity and health at Spa Samui. Thanks to my affirmations, the friendship gods smiled down on me when I met two fellow Canadians, Sarah and Melissa. We'd met briefly a few days earlier at a Muay Thai boxing match and, because of the home-land connection, became instant friends. Within an hour of getting to know each other, we decided to meet up a few days later on Koh Phangnan. I was beyond grateful that my new friends let me bunk with them as rooms were sold out island-wide in anticipation of the full moon party. Otherwise, I may have had to involuntarily experience camping excursion number two.

On our first night in Koh Phangnan, the three of us ventured to Haad Rin where we'd heard a variety of festivities were taking place. We were ready to partake in some preliminary full moon party good times.

Honestly, I think the motivation for setting up some of the entertainment is purely to see how ridiculous the drunken tourists can get. When booze is involved, rational-thinking goes out the window and bad decisions naturally follow. Thailand provided the perfect setting for these scenarios to take place. A prime example was when one of the bars had a nearly fifteen-foot long skipping rope doused in gasoline and set on fire for people to jump through. Was I in party heaven or hell? Wherever I was, the line between the two was thin.

The combination of booze flowing freely and the novelty of such an activity drew people in. Massive line-ups formed for this unusual version of double-dutch, where the mental wellness of the rope-turners was definitely in question. I can't begin to count the number of health and safety laws that must have been broken. Tourists were literally nose-diving into the fire. How was that even a method of skipping? For many, what seemed like a good idea at the time was a probable regret the next day, with the discovery of singed arm hair or burnt clothing. This was one experience I knew well-enough not to participate in. It was an interesting introduction to this infamous island, which presented me with a vastly different experience than that of Spa Samui.

Koh Phangnan is a fantastically unique little island with a charm of its own. While hints of traditional Thai culture echo here and there, it has been globalized and tailored to tourist interests. There's the full moon party once a month, where it seems that every day is either spent in preparation mode or in recovery mode. Another fun little quirk is that episodes of *Friends* and *Family Guy* play on loop on the television sets in the restaurants. I enjoyed this tremendously.

After several days of acquainting myself with Koh Phangnan, watching multiple episodes of *Friends*, and getting to know my new roommates, Sarah and Melissa, the full moon party was upon us. I could feel the excitement in the air. The vibe of the Island was fueled by adrenaline and a touch of lunacy. I was fired up to party after being Zen for the past week.

In general, one of my favourite parts of "going out" is the pre-party process. This is when random stories of partying-past come out, 90s dance and hip-hop tunes are pumping, and the drinks are flowing. Impromptu playful dance parties form naturally, and the departure time for the bar gets pushed back. More often than not, the pre-party turns out to be the best part of the evening.

I'm a strong believer in arriving at the bar fashionably late, as it tends to pale in comparison to the pre-party fun. The destination of the bar is simply an excuse for the party to take place.

When I do finally arrive at the bar, I like to make a grand entrance and urge my friends to walk in laughing. This makes us look fun, approachable, and like the group of friends you want to party with. Inevitably, through our playful laughter, we wind up producing true laughter that heightens the group's energy, so it's a win-win. It's cheesy, but it totally works—my favourite kind of mini-life lesson. The pre-party with Sarah and Melissa did not disappoint. We purchased our pre-drinks at the local 7-Eleven, which are ubiquitous in Thailand, and cleverly poured them into over-sized ketchup and mustard bottles. We brought the bottles to the beach party, where they not only served as a conversation starter, but also kept the sand out of our drinks for the entire night—so clever!

We also picked up glow-in-the-dark body paint to decorate ourselves for the festivities. I mixed the colours onto our paper plate palette and as I was about to apply the first brush stroke onto my arm, an odd hesitation halted me. What was I doing? I'm an adult. Adults don't paint on themselves. Adults shouldn't be this silly. I'd been flowing with the silliness of the evening, but all of a sudden I became rational. And with that, my energy shifted. With my reluctance came negativity, and with that negativity came discomfort. I needed to shake this off!

I thought about it.

When was the last time I could creatively paint on myself and walk around in public and it wouldn't be frowned upon? When I was ten?

I was having so much fun embracing the playfulness—why choose to stop?

I reconnected to my open mind, loving heart mantra and re-tapped into the playful zone in which I'd been having so much fun. I did a quick kick-ball-change, and went for it. I chose a vibrant purple paint and drew a whimsical loop surrounded by hearts across my forearm. The three of us took turns painting different images and shapes on each other's hard-to-reach places and laughed the entire time. Why didn't I do things like this more often?

By participating in this silly and fun activity, I'd tapped into my inner child. My imagination was flowing and I wasn't worried about all the "stuff" that usually gets in the way of having true, raw, goofy fun.

BE PLAYFUL

When you give into your child-like sense of playfulness, you emit positive energy. Being playful yields immediate results in the quest for happiness. In a way, you recapture that innocent sense of wonder and simplistic appreciation.

My time in Thailand had an underlying theme of being playful and having fun. By connecting with that side of myself, I temporarily let go of the constraints of adulthood. Playfulness is at the core of who we are and brings us back to the state of wonderment and joy we had as children. When we were kids, we found any reason to laugh and amuse ourselves. Laughter releases endorphins, which in turn make us happy. Children are constantly on the quest to laugh, have fun, and be happy. Why aren't we?

Our minds fall victim to routines, beating on the same frequency and staying in tune with what's secure and expected. We focus on our careers, responsibilities, and the "shoulds" that form in our adult life. Our mindsets become staid and rigid.

Yes, it's wise to acknowledge responsibilities and personal safety, but it's also wise to connect to that voice within—the youthful, uncomplicated version of yourself that hasn't been conditioned by external stresses of adulthood. By breaking out of your routines and incorporating playfulness and fun, you allow your mind to soar into a nostalgic, happy territory. You return to your inner child.

Sometimes, when nobody is looking, I'll do a cartwheel or a grand jeté (leaping split) to get from point A to B, just because it's fun and also funny. If I'm feeling proud of myself, as a personal reward, I'll burst into a hand-clapping gypsy dance to boost my mood even higher (Ang Urquhart loves when people clap in circles). These silly actions amuse me and the only consequence is happiness.

CALL TO ACTION

Don't take yourself so seriously! Let go of the barriers created over the years and allow yourself to reach a natural essence of your being. Take a break from caring about criticism, the stresses of your everyday life, the pressures of work, or looking silly by adding a little bit of a hop or a shuffle to your steps. With this attunement to your inner child, you'll feel free.

Here are some examples of what you can do right now to tap into your inner child and be playful:

Have a dance party. Right now! Do it!

Instead of walking from point A to point B, do the grapevine, skip, or prance.

Colour! Get crayons, paints, pencil crayons, and create fun and beautiful images!

Blow bubbles.

When you go to bed tonight, make a pillow fort.

Go for ice cream!

Play on the swings or the teeter-totter at the park. (Find an equally playful friend for this.)

Think about what you used to do as a child and do what brought you immediate happiness. Simple actions of a child bring infinite amounts of joy.

LIFE LESSON EIGHTEEN: BE KIND TO YOUR SERVER

"Remember there's no such thing as a small act of kindness. Every act creates a ripple with no logical end."
—Scott Adams, Creator of the Dilbert Comic Strip

In Thailand, I had no choice but to adopt patience, humility, and a bit of comedic appreciation to enjoy a meal. The morning after the full moon party, the girls and I decided to feast our ravenously hungry (and hungover) selves at a Thai-Mexican restaurant we'd discovered a few days earlier. Shamefully, my days of detoxification were a distant memory. I planned to reconnect with Life Lesson Thirteen: Eat Mindfully, as soon as my booze flu passed. Nachos were the escape route.

When ordering food in Thailand, you basically have to roll the dice and hope for the best possible outcome. A language barrier is almost always present, so special requests or adding to whatever's on the menu brings you into risky territory.

Feeling the after-effects of the full moon party, we emerged from our guesthouse and dragged our dehydrated, sorry-looking selves to the outdoor patio down the street. The concrete structure painted in a kaleidoscope of colours resembled a restaurant in an all-inclusive Mexican resort with the usual classic sombreros and piñatas. However, it was also lined with glistening golden Buddhas. The décor lacked focus, but I loved it.

Whenever I feel lethargic and hungry after an evening out on the town, I crave nachos and lots of them. It doesn't even matter what time of the day it is. Luckily, nachos were one of the three listed Mexican menu items. The rest, all Thai. This randomness delighted me and the ensuing laughter served to remedy my hangover.

The petite Thai waitress softly shuffled up to our table and we ordered three large plates of nachos. No chance any of us were sharing that day.

I requested to have the sour cream served on the side, instead of on top of the nachos, as listed on the menu.

Our server responded, "No, sorry. It's at the pier."

We weren't quite sure what that meant, but decided to move forward. Instead, we requested guacamole.

She replied, "No, that's finished."

I thought to myself, *Hmmm... This is getting a bit challenging.* We tried one last time by asking for extra salsa to compensate for the lack of variety in dipping products. She happily answered, "Yes,", but in the end, brought over a bottle of ketchup.

Bless her cute heart.

I happen to be extremely particular when it comes to eating at restaurants. I'm every server's nightmare because I almost always modify my meal. "No red onions please," or "Add spinach to the dish," or "Can you substitute avocado for the bacon, swap out the mozzarella for light Swiss cheese, and add a honey dijon instead of mayo?"

I rarely want exactly what's listed on the menu. I know it's annoying. I also know it'll likely take more organization on the server's end, and at times my order may not be accurate. I take it with a grain of salt and a touch of patience, so my experience is generally enjoyable.

In Thailand, not only was I modifying according to the Ang mode of food design, but I had to contend with a language barrier. Things didn't go as planned and that was okay! The cool thing was, I wasn't annoyed by it.

Maybe it was partly due to the hangover, but I was able to appreciate being in a position where I could receive customer service. Was it the server's fault the sour cream was at the pier? Probably not. Was it her fault she confused ketchup for salsa? No. It was miscommunication.

Some elements of customer service at the restaurant didn't exactly meet my expectations for the optimum dining experience, but in the grand scheme of things it didn't really matter. What does matter is how we react to these small challenges in our daily interactions.

At the end of our interesting Mexican-Thai feast, I took a moment to thank our teeny tiny server. I walked over to her, gave the Wai greeting, and with sincerity, explained how much we enjoyed our experience and her lovely service. She again apologized for the lack of dipping products, and, much to my surprise, gave me a hug. I hugged her back, wanting to embrace her forever!

Even though our food was a little suspicious, the experience in general was enjoyable, and because of my kindness towards our server, I was rewarded with a hug.

BE KIND TO YOUR SERVER

We're all part of a karmic exchange that begins with the basic relationships we create with the people we meet every day. How we deal with these people speaks to our true character, demonstrating who we are.

Whether it's a server, a barista at a local coffee shop, or a bus driver on a morning commute, you're constantly presented with interactions where your inherent goodness can shine through. By showing kindness, you demonstrate basic human decency to someone who's there to be of service to you and take care of your needs. When you recognize innate worth in another and show them respect, you align with your best self. You'll feel good when you extend kindness to those who provide a service.

CALL TO ACTION

Next time you go out to dine, be kind to your server. That person could be a college student trying to make ends meet, a future artist making just enough to get by, or a little Thai girl who just wants to be of good service to guests.

You can show kindness to your server, or other people in service, by doing one or a combination of the following:

Show interest in and appreciation for your server. Ask their name. Ask them thoughtful questions. Express gratitude and show courtesy. Manners have magical effects.

If you need to complain about something, be nice about it. Chances are, it wasn't the server who prepared the meal and made the mistake. And chances are, it can be easily fixed.

Tip. It's another simple form of karma, and the exchange of money for services rendered is a way to balance out the universe.

Enjoy yourself! This energy radiates and is contagious.

LIFE LESSON NINETEEN:
HAVE A "YOU" DAY

*"Make sure you take the time to feed yourself with what your spirit
has to offer."*
–Darren L. Johnson

After curing my full moon party hangover with nachos, my time
in Thailand was almost complete. I said goodbye to Sarah and
Melissa after exchanging Facebook details and telephone numbers,
pledging to stay in touch after we returned to Canada. Boarding the
overnight bus (after yet another ferry ride) to my aunt's apartment
in Bangkok, I was once again on my own.

The travel visa in Thailand is valid for one month. If you exit
the country and return, the visa is re-stamped and you can stay for
another month. My end date was looming, so I chose to continue
onwards and downwards in my travels, booking a flight to Australia.
With only one day remaining in Thailand, I decided to spend my
final hours soaking up as much Thai culture as I could.

I woke up at the respectable hour of 8:00 a.m. (Ang Urquhart
does not like early mornings), and visited the local market for fresh
tropical fruit and coffee. I leisurely strolled up and down the rows
of food vendors, smiling at everyone and showcasing the Wai greeting. Sawadee-kahs all around! Right there, I made a silent vow to
introduce the Wai greeting to my friends in Canada.

With my cup of coffee half full (much like my outlook on life), I made my way to a charming little Internet café to sit back, enjoy my delicious coffee, post my latest travel blog, and catch up on global issues (and by global issues I mean celebrity gossip on Perez Hilton—my guilty pleasure).

After a few minutes of mindlessly scrolling through the website and familiarizing myself with the latest celebrity antics, I explored the surrounding neighbourhood where I happily stumbled upon an Olympic-sized swimming pool. Since it was 90 degrees celsius outside, I decided to cool off and work out before my flight to Australia, so I purchased a day pass. After 10 laps of elementary backstroke, my body was screaming for a massage, and what better place than Thailand to get a full body massage for only $6?

The massage gave me time to think about what to do next. I was leaving for Australia early the following day, but (as usual) hadn't solidified my game plan. I desperately needed to call Gianni, my friend I was going to stay with, but I couldn't figure out how to make international calls from a payphone. The instructions were listed in Thai, and the three basic phrases I knew (all of which involved ordering drinks) were useless. I was 30 minutes away from downtown Bangkok and almost no one spoke English, so I was unable to receive assistance.

While my verbal foreign language skills may have been terrible, I've always been good at using non-verbal communication tools. I returned to the Internet café and attempted to convey my dilemma to the lovely girl working there. Through an artistic form of sign language and a touch of modern jazz (which included a barrel-turn somehow), she was able to identify that I needed to make a phone call. With absolute generosity (and probably a touch of pity), she offered me the use of her personal cell phone so I could call my friend!

Once I made plans and finished the phone call, I was hungry. Marvelously, this caring girl continued to extend kindness and ordered a cheese pizza for us to share at the Internet café. I reclined back into one of the fantastic beanbag chairs that decorated the cafe, kicked my feet up, and streamed an episode of my favourite television show, *The Office*, while enjoying a slice of pizza. Just as I thought I couldn't be happier with the current state of events, my new Thai friend gifted me a Thai Christmas ornament! Her kindness elevated my mood to even higher levels.

As I sat back smiling, I realized I'd unintentionally just experienced one of my favourite days: an Ang Day.

HAVE A "YOU" DAY

Back home, I'd make plans to have Ang Days on a regular basis. These are guilt-free days where anything goes, as long as I'm happy with and actively embracing my choices. From early on, I knew taking time for myself was necessary to create balance. This was most apparent when I worked as a wedding planner and donated an enormous amount of energy to others and their happiness. To give that energy, I needed to take care of myself first. So, on this self-proclaimed day of restoration and self-care, I made the agreement that the day would revolve only around activities I wanted to do.

In Canada, a typical Ang Day might involve splurging on a mani-pedi while enjoying a sinful coffee with sugar, whipped cream and sprinkles. Other days might include treating myself to a new accessory or going for a solitary walk outdoors. My favourite of all Ang Days involved a trip to my former dance studio, blasting music, and busting out an impromptu dance routine (involving leaping splits and outrageous handstand maneuvers).

Sometimes you just have to be selfish and concentrate on yourself. This allows you to decompress from the hustle and bustle of everyday life. It relaxes your mind by enjoying some of the simple or not-so-simple life pleasures. Marilyn Monroe said it beautifully, "I restore myself when I'm alone."

CALL TO ACTION

Focus all your attention inward and embark on a daytime journey of rejuvenation and fun. Unapologetically follow through with your favourite guilty pleasures and bask in an aura of personal satisfaction. Plan a date with yourself. Here's how:

Look at your calendar and pick a day. Plan nothing on this day except for time with yourself.

Plot a few activities that will bring you happiness. Is it a trip to your favourite park? A venture to the local bookstore to get lost in the titles of inspiring books? Is it a yoga class? Make a plan.

Wake up that day with a feeling of empowerment. Be playful (refer back to Life Lesson Seventeen) and do a fun little morning dance to set the tone for the day.

Smile often throughout the day.

Keep a notepad to mark down feelings of gratitude. Take pictures with your phone throughout the day. Observe your awesome life through notes you write and photos you capture.

Have "You" days often and infuse them with more creativity each time!

LIFE LESSON TWENTY: KEEP
IN TOUCH WITH FRIENDS

"A friend is one of the nicest things you can have, and one of the
nicest things you can be."
–Douglas Pagels

As I left Bangkok and boarded the plane for Australia, I reflected on my month spent in Thailand—the places I saw and the people I met. My travels thus far allowed me to meet new friends from all over the world. Some, I'll likely never see again. Others, I stay in touch with via social media. Then there are those I text with, talk to, or even travel with occasionally.

While in Australia, my approach with friends shifted from making new ones to reconnecting with ones I already had. My arrival would reunite me with one of my good friends from university, Gianni.

Gianni graciously offered to pick me up from the airport in Brisbane and had even agreed to let me to crash on his couch in a town called Mooloolaba (best word) on the Sunshine Coast. "Sunshine Coast" is seriously the perfect name for this place, unless of course, it was named "Loving Life Coast." It's located on a white sandy beach with emerald waters, and the weather is warm and sunny with a cloudless sky every day—who wouldn't love life there?

The last time Gianni and I saw one another had been two years earlier when we met for dinner while he was home from one of one of his many travel adventures. He'd left Canada soon after university to play pro basketball around the world. From Italy to Ireland to the Canary Islands, Gianni was a seasoned traveller. We had kept in touch via MSN (throwback!) and Facebook every now and then, but we'd never gone so far as to pick up the phone.

So, while I considered him my friend, if we were both in Canada, I doubt I would have gone and visited him for a week. However, in the spirit of travel, an invitation to stay at a friend's place on the other side of the world is a hot ticket, especially in Australia where the cost of accommodations is far more inflated than in Thailand.

I arrived at the airport in Brisbane feeling volumes better than when I'd arrived in Thailand. I had my luggage safe with me, I was a half a bottle of Australian wine deep due to the free wine offered on the flight, and I was excited to see a familiar face. As I made my way out of the airport and into the sunshine, I squinted as I scanned the pick-up area. From about 20 ft. away, I heard the recognizable shout of my name. After two years, here we stood reunited on the other side of the world.

For a tall guy (6 ft., 7 in), he drove a comically tiny vehicle. With both of us squashed into the front seat and my backpack in the back, I felt like I was seated in some hilarious clown car. During the one-hour ride from the airport to Gianni's place in Mooloolaba, we caught each other up on the past few years. It's crazy when you spend time with someone you haven't seen in years and are able to instantly and seamlessly pick up right where you left off. I had forgotten how much I appreciated Gianni and his company.

My introduction to the Aussie lifestyle far exceeded any expectations I had. My days began with a solitary walk along the beach, where the radiant energy of the sun and calming sound of the waves fueled my inspiration to write. I selected a perfect spot on the beach and transformed my thoughts into journal entries and blog posts.

Afternoons were spent with Gianni's surfer friend learning how to ride the waves (sort of). Most of the time, surfing meant me resting on the surfboard, floating along the water and tanning. My surf instructor wasn't impressed. To balance out an afternoon of relaxation, I'd go for a quick run and complete a yoga practice before dinner. By night, I enjoyed the stars from Gianni's backyard, which was set along the water. I was on the Sunshine Coast of Australia with a smile stretched so wide across my face my cheeks hurt. "Loving Life Coast", indeed!

What truly lifted my spirits during my first few days in Australia was reconnecting with an old friend. There was never a dull conversation, and it was fantastic to see him living a happy life in Australia. By reconnecting on the Sunshine Coast, I learned so many new and wonderful things about Gianni. It deepened our friendship in a way that wouldn't have happened had I not made the effort to reach out and reconnect.

Joyously, I prolonged this life lesson, as my next stop took me to the epicentre of Australia: Sydney. There, I'd reconnect with another friend from my university days, Laura.

KEEP IN TOUCH WITH FRIENDS

When I was a child, I persistently asked to hang out with my friends no matter what the weather was like or what obligations we had as a family or what school work needed to be completed. I was never too busy for my friends. My mission then is my mission now: I must nourish my friendships because they directly link to my level of happiness.

As adults, we tend to distance ourselves from this mission and fall victim to the phrase, "I'm so busy." Life is busy. Life is filled with exhausting, exciting, and stressful events, all of which equate to a "busy" existence. Sometimes we make ourselves busy with things that serve no purpose or things that do nothing to uplift us. Sometimes we are busy with obligations and circumstances beyond our control.

This hectic lifestyle makes staying in touch with friends all the more challenging. When you don't see someone on a regular basis, it requires more effort, which can be a tricky element to nourishing friendships. When you do offer energy to reconnecting, you bring yourself to that happy social place where your friendship lies.

By focusing on this friendship component, you preserve the part of your soul that contains your collective memories. You nourish the social part of your personal makeup that has shaped you over the years. Your friends are people who have shared common interests, memories, and experiences. They're part of your personal history.

CALL TO ACTION

Whether they're your next-door neighbour or a friend on the other side of the world, maintaining positive relationships provides joy in your life. Is there a friend who holds a warm place in your heart, but you haven't spoken with in a long time?

Here's what you can do right now to reconnect:

Send a Facebook message. These days, the opportunity to reconnect is easier than ever. Think about how you feel when someone you haven't chatted with in a while reaches out to see how you're doing. I know I feel great!

Set up a friend-date. Make plans to go for a coffee or better yet, a glass of wine. Rehash old memories in person and share some laughs.

Plan a mini-reunion. Remember that favourite group of people you pre-drank with every weekend in university? Have an anniversary edition of that amazing time in your life. Plan a gathering that gives you something to look forward to and the opportunity to reconnect with a number of long-lost friends.

LIFE LESSON TWENTY-ONE: CHERISH YOUR MEMORIES

"Memory is a way of holding onto the things you love, the things you are, the things you never want to lose."
–Kevin Arnold, The Wonder Years

After a gloriously warm week in December on Loving Life Coast, I set out for my next Australian destination. I arrived in Sydney late on December 23rd, where I was greeted by another one of my university friends, Laura, and a bottle of wine—both of which made me smile. The unofficial underlying theme of Australia, reconnecting with friends, was going strong and I couldn't have asked for a better place to have university reunions.

My first full day in Sydney happened to be Christmas Eve, so Laura and I put ourselves in the holiday spirit by touring downtown and taking pictures with various Christmas trees. As we made our way to the main square, I realized it was my first Christmas without snow. Hearing Christmas carols echoing in the streets and seeing storefronts decorated with holly berries, garland, and snowflakes, while wearing shorts and a tube-top seemed surreal. Back home in Canada, the weather was below zero, so I welcomed the juxtaposition of Christmas elements in Australia.

When we returned from our walking tour of the city, Laura took me to her friends' (and by association my new friends'), Shannon and Mitra's, apartment for a home-cooked Christmas Eve dinner. After dining at restaurants and greasy food carts for the past month, it was a treat to have a meal prepared with love in a beautiful and clean kitchen.

Mitra has a natural talent for cooking and decided to prepare one of her traditional Persian dishes called Kuku (similar to the Italian dish frittata, which is similar to a big delicious omelet). This magnificent meal made me reminisce about the times I enjoyed a similar egg feast at family functions. I reflected on holiday traditions spent with my family, and again, felt that pang of sadness from missing everyone back home, especially my Nonno.

One of my most cherished memories is my Nonno cooking frittata, which was typically done only at Easter. However, on our last Christmas together, somehow frittata made its way into the succession of Christmas meals, going against the seasonality of meals my grandparents had rigidly preached my entire life.

At the time, I didn't know why we were breaking the all-powerful Italian food rules, but we enjoyed the year-round specialty meals over the course of two days. I still wonder to this day if on some level, he knew it would be his last Christmas.

Every December 24th, I celebrated Christmas Eve by having dinner at my Nonno and Nonna's house. Our particular family tradition was to have 12 different food items for dinner, most of which were seafood. This elaborate fish banquet was referred to as Cena di Vigilia. Why it was 12 items, I'm not sure. What I was sure of is they were 12 of my least favourite food items possible.

My grandparent's house on Christmas Eve emitted a foul stench that will forever be engrained in my memory: a combination of chi-chi and baccala (stinky salted cod fish), smelts (even stinkier, smaller fish), and whatever additional new fish dish my Nonno read about from the recipes in the magazines he would steal from the doctor's office (he wasn't a clepto, but he was frugal and felt it was his right to take the magazines, as they were available at his disposal).

I usually brought my own grocery-bought pizza to eat instead of this fish feast, which angered my Nonno greatly.

When I gingerly approached my Nonno to preheat the oven to bake my pizza, he had no hesitation unleashing the Italian guilt on me. First, I got the long, exaggerated "sigh" (and I'd question how long he could, in fact, hold his breath). Next, he clasped his hands and shook them back and forth in a prayer form saying, "You no want na-thing. Dio mio, Dio mio." (In Italian, this means, "My God, my God.") Finally, he tried to bargain with me, offering to heat my pizza if I sampled one of his 12 dishes. I always agreed to this final request, but then hid the little fish morsel underneath a piece of bread on my plate, careful not to hurt his feelings.

This was my typical Christmas Eve routine. Although it wasn't my favourite meal, it was a gathering I cherished regardless of my dislike of the food. My Nonno created an environment that, although stinky, was filled with love and family appreciation, and for that reason I'm forever grateful.

My Nonno focused his gratitude on three specific things. First, he placed the utmost importance on his family. Family was the main motivator in every action he took, and he cherished all the times we were together—at the dinner table, at local festivals, or family celebrations. He would be proud that his family continues to live by his example and cherishes every memory we have of him.

Second, he placed importance on religion and his Catholic faith. He believed in God. He believed in living a good life as a person of faith and thanking God for his blessings.

And third, as you may have already guessed, was the importance of food. He put thought and care into every meal, and we always prayed to express our gratitude for the bounty in front of us.

On the morning of December 25th, I had the last meal my Nonno would ever prepare for me: frittata. I reflect on that Christmas morning and cherish the monumental effort he took in preparing a meal. He was grateful he could host us at his home, and at the start of our meals led the family in prayer, where he always cried because of his profound gratitude. Everything about that last breakfast spent around the family table was perfect. We enjoyed the elaborate egg dish in each other's company, laughed, and told stories. It's a memory I'll always cherish. He had the stroke a few days after Christmas.

Although I was on other side of the world on Christmas Eve one year later, I felt comforted in celebrating the holiday with a similar food dish to my Nonno's. This was a different Christmas for me. It was the first Christmas without my beloved Nonno, and the first Christmas away from my family and friends. Christmas in Australia allowed me to reflect on the wonderful experiences I'd had and be happy about those times.

It's this reflection— looking back on the memories with my friends and family—that reminds me I live a blessed life. Taking time to reflect and cherish my memories is the life lesson I learned from experiencing Christmas in a new way.

CHERISH YOUR MEMORIES

There's not a day that goes by where I don't think about my Nonno. I'd give everything I have just to have another five minutes with him. Even though I miss him, thinking of him makes me happy. He instilled the importance of family, tradition, and gratefulness within me—and for that, I'm fortunate.

With his loss, I know that Christmas has been forever changed. After reflecting on the life lessons from my Nonno, I can approach all holidays with an open mind and loving heart and accept new traditions. He gave me the gift of years of great memories, and his influence has shaped the way I am today. As corny or cheesy as it sounds, I know he was looking down on me during my travels and clasping his hands back and forth in prayer form, saying "Dio mio," but with a big gap-toothed smile on his face.

When you cherish something, you infuse it with positivity, thus engaging your best self. Reflecting on your past experiences allows a sentimental feeling of nostalgia to occur, associating you with a time or place when happy events occurred. Once again, you place yourself in a position of gratitude, elevating your spirit.

CALL TO ACTION

Take time to embrace the traditions you have with your family and reflect on the good times. Here are some ways to keep the memories alive:

Get together with relatives often and retell stories. Share stories with people who can relate.

Reminisce about family customs.

Share favourite moments.

Embrace traditions and create your own.

Go through old photo albums. Look for the intention in those pictures and appreciate the value embedded in them.

Feel nostalgic.

Allow yourself to live in the moment so you can create more memories. Put down your cell phone and be engaged in the present. Enjoy the simplicity of spending time with family and friends.

LIFE LESSON TWENTY-TWO:
SPEND TIME WITH ANIMALS

*"Petting, scratching, and cuddling a dog could be as soothing to the
mind and heart as deep meditation and almost as good for the soul
as prayer."*
—Dean Koontz

After spending Christmas Day on the beach, I was ready to
channel my touristy side and participate in some authentic
Australian activities. When Laura suggested the popular Wine and
Wildlife day tour, I instantly registered. The tour group met the next
day at 7:00 a.m. a few blocks away from Laura's apartment. Usually,
the early morning factor would make me dismiss an activity, but
with wine as the end-game, I agreed to go.

At 6:45 the next morning, with my eyes not fully opened, I
collected my registration kit. Fifteen other participants and I prepared to make our way to one of the most famous wine regions in
Australia, the Hunter Valley.

The tour began with a visit to a wildlife park where we would
learn about the animals indigenous to Australia. In a way, I felt that
my whole life had been leading up to meeting a koala bear. When
we finally arrived at the koala sanctuary, I could barely contain
my excitement!

ANGELA URQUHART

I lined up to take my photo with a koala, choosing to stage it with the yoga posture "tree pose." It seemed appropriate given the setting. I rooted my left foot firmly into the earth, bent my right knee and pressed the sole of my foot into my standing leg, arms stretched above me, mimicking the trunk and branches of the koala's eucalyptus tree.

As I looked at the koala perched in the fork of the tree, I noticed how relaxed he was. Because koalas eat the leaves of a eucalyptus tree all day, which contributes to a high-fiber, low-nutrient diet, they have a slow metabolic rate and are constantly sleepy. The relaxed demeanor of the koalas made me smile. From the positive vibes they exuded, my little koala friends left me feeling joyful and by imitation, pretty chilled out.

After a few moments of yoga poses and selfies with my new koala friend, I was directed to move on so the next person could have their turn. I sat on a bench, still within sight of the koala, and I began to feel nostalgic about my childhood pet, our family dog named Buddy.

Growing up, my brother and I were lucky enough to have a pet. It must have been divine fate that brought this big, goofy Golden Retriever, so full of personality, into our home. Somehow, Buddy possessed the dramatics in dog form that I held in human form. He lived big and with his heart. He also lived with a mind of his own. Puppy school and our many attempts at obedience training were wildly unsuccessful. He was a troublemaker, but his motivation was to seek attention. At nine years old, I could relate.

Every morning before school, when my next-door neighbour, Reggie, picked me up, Buddy would dart past us out the door for his daily self-proclaimed run. Perhaps he was searching for some "me time," taking notes from his Dramatically Zen sister.

Each day, the same sequence of events would repeat. Buddy galloped down the street, looking back and taunting us with a large, mischievous smile. I followed him, running as fast as I could while my brother pedaled on his bike in high pursuit. My mom joined in, speeding down the street in the family van, all of us part of a magical parade chasing a massive Golden Retriever through the neighbour-hood. Typically, this lasted about 10 to 15 minutes, at which time Buddy would forfeit his chase. His attention-seeking mission had been accomplished. And each day, I would go to school slightly sweaty and with a cramp in my side.

The thing is, we could never truly be or stay mad at Buddy. When he would gaze up at us with those big eyes and goofy grin (and somehow an oddly apologetic expression), our anger was replaced by love and appreciation. My irritation dissipated almost instantly when Buddy returned home, wagged his tail, and scooted his head underneath my hand so I could pet him. Three seconds later, I'd find myself hugging him and cooing over him, forgetting I'd been angry in the first place. He just had that affect on me.

Following my photo session with the koala bear, I felt a similar appreciation resurface for being in the company of an animal friend. I reflected on my own happy experiences with the most dramatic, yet lovable, pet in Buddy and found synchronicity by enjoying the company of a koala bear.

SPEND TIME WITH ANIMALS

Animals have a joyful presence, which magically transforms the entire energy of a room to a happier space. When you're around them, you feel good. It's that simple.

Have you ever noticed that when you address a pet your vocal tone changes to a more upbeat, playful one? It's interesting to watch people talk to animals, as they become engaged in "happy talk." When I was face-to-face with the koala bears, I spoke to them as though they could fully understand what I was saying. My voice rose two octaves higher and infused with an operatic tone. Animals make us want to create a happy dialogue, since being in their loveable presence immediately sets this tone. As evidence points out, when you smile and inject your speech with positivity, you feel more positive.

In nursing homes, therapy dogs are brought in to uplift the residents' spirits. These dogs are trained to be in this type of social environment and their mission is to provide a calming presence.

The motion of petting animals is a form of massage, a process that relaxes the animal, which then becomes part of an exchange, and the petter becomes relaxed too. There's scientific evidence showing that petting animals helps to not only lower blood pressure, but also produces endorphins that brings happiness and blocks pain. These playful pooches spread joy to those who need it most.

Author George Eliot identified the positive contribution that animals, specifically dogs, bring into our lives, describing them as agreeable friends. They ask no questions, they pass no judgments. They love you for you and nothing else. It's an unconditional love filled with gratitude. Spending time with animals is one of the most basic, simple, and genuine relationships in the world.

CALL TO ACTION

The stress-free aura that animals radiate is contagious, so place yourself in the company of a dog, cat, koala bear, or even a llama.

Spend time with animals! If you don't own a pet, ask your friendly neighbour to take their dog for a walk (a little karmic exchange at its best), or visit a local petting zoo. As a last resort, browse cute puppy pictures online.

Your mood will be lifted immediately.

LIFE LESSON TWENTY-THREE: SET INTENTIONS

"Intentions compressed into words enfold magical power."
–Deepak Chopra

After making friends with a koala bear, I also formed new friendships with a kangaroo and a very large, and likely very old, turtle, therefore achieving my tourist-aspirations for the week in Australia. Once our wildlife park visit was complete, the tour took our group to five wineries where I felt it was appropriate to purchase a bottle of wine at each. With New Year's Eve just a few days away, I wanted to properly stock up.

New Year's Eve had never been one of my favourite celebrations, but with five bottles of Australian wine and the memory of fluffy koalas lingering, the build up to New Year's Eve had so far surpassed previous years.

Oh the dilemma of New Year's Eve plans. It's a predicament we've all experienced at one point. It's the biggest party night of the year that connects the entire world—all part of a massive shift from one year to the next. It's a night to toast the great memories of the past year, let go of the not-so-great memories and, of course, start anew. Unfortunately, New Year's Eve has always been anti-climactic for me.

For years, my friends and I made the concerted effort to avoid the inevitable New Year's Eve let-down by attempting to create exciting plans in advance. We would brainstorm events that included, but weren't limited to, a house party, a night out at a club, or even a casual movie and pig-out night in. Inevitably though, someone would bail out, get sick or change their mind about the evening's venue at the last minute, and plans would become discombobulated. Our high hopes for New Year's Eve would almost always turn out to be mediocre.

The aftermath was always followed by a series of self-proclaimed "fixes" in the form of the elusive New Year's resolution. The words "fix" and "resolution" denote that something is wrong. First, we'd have a ho-hum evening, then the next day we'd talk about everything we needed to change. For me, all of this equated to just wanting to get the night over with.

But I was in Australia this year, so it was time to let go of my preconceived notions about New Year's Eve. Instead, I was going to focus on this awesome one with an open mind and a loving heart. I would transform my negative thoughts into positive intentions. I had to redirect my mind to a more favourable course.

With that, I came up with a fresh perspective and boldly declared, "I am celebrating New Year's Eve in Sydney, Australia, and it will be nothing short of epic."

December 31st started on the highest note. Embracing our Dramatically Zen side, Laura and I soaked up the sun on the rooftop terrace of her apartment building, sipping sparkling wine, and noshing on fresh homemade guacamole and tortilla chips. Afterwards, a group of us, a fusion of fantastically interesting people from countries all around the world (including Nepal, Ireland, Luxembourg, and Armenia), made our way to Sydney Harbour, which was *the* place in Australia to celebrate.

An estimated 1.5 million people gathered in the Harbour around the famous Opera House to ring in the new year. Using my keen ability to bypass lines at all costs, we meandered our way past the enormous lineup and throngs of people to claim the perfect spot to view the midnight fireworks.

While this seemed incredibly marvelous and magical as we pre-pared for the new year, the realization of our situation finally struck us, and my New Year's Eve curse returned to haunt me. We arrived at 5:00 p.m. and secured a prime location for the fireworks, but we'd failed to consider what we'd do until midnight and hadn't packed food or drinks for the seven-hour wait. Hot off the heels of being an event planner extraordinaire, how could I not have planned better? I usually have a three-course picnic packed for an outing to the movies.

The only food stand nearby was a questionable German fast food vendor with a two-hour wait that even my line-bypassing skills couldn't crack.

I wandered around our viewing area and searched for an area to purchase a glass of wine to ease my troubled nerves. This was when our night reached a pathetic, yet hilarious, level that we did not see coming: we were stuck in the gated-in, alcohol-free "family zone." My vision of having a cocktail to ring in the new year dissolved.

Much like the scene at the airport in Thailand, lost luggage and all, these things were out of my control. What I could control, though, was my reaction to it. So, I laughed it off (which sounded more like a mad scientist's laugh) and danced my way back to our spot.

I initially thought the lack of alcohol would be devastating to my New Year's Eve fun, but who knew I didn't need alcohol to have a good time? I'd set the intention of having an epic evening, and dammit, I was going to have it. Our small group of international friends added something unique and entertaining to the conver-sation, and the seven hours flew by. We took the opportunity to people-watch, and I loved observing the happiness on people's faces as the countdown to midnight inched closer. I set aside my former notion of the New Year's Eve let-down as the crowd's energy brought me to a new, exciting place. The element of fun was simply present.

At long last, the midnight hour was upon us. We had heard that $5 million was spent on the fireworks display and it was the biggest one the world had seen since the turn of the millenium in 2000. To have a front row seat was something I'd never dreamed I'd experience. Fireworks were set off all around us—over Sydney Harbor Bridge, the Opera House, the buildings behind us, and the barges in the water. A myriad of colours exploded in the night sky and danced with songs playing over loudspeakers throughout the harbour front. The booming of the fireworks heightened the bass in the music.

The energy from the crowd was palpable. My skin crawled with excitement and my heart fluttered with joy. The cheering and celebrating during the first 20 minutes of the new year was better than I could've expected. The tone for my upcoming year was set. I made a silent vow that the positive energy I was feeling would carry on throughout the year.

Later in the evening, the 1.5 million spectators flooded the downtown streets. Laura and I made our way to a house party where we downed a bottle of bubbly as fast as humanly possible. I then proceeded to call everyone back home whose phone numbers I remembered. It was New Year's Day, but back home, it was still New Year's Eve morning, which meant I was calling from a different year! So sci-fi! While I did rack up over $100 in cell phone charges, I have no regrets.

The commencement of the new year began on a positive tone— one I decided to embrace throughout the remainder of the year. I declared it, "The Year of Ang." My purpose was to live with the intention I had set for my travels. I would embrace an open mind and loving heart, and make every attempt to be the best version of myself.

To me, intentions equate to possibilities, opportunities, and having a positive outlook. "New Year's resolution" seems to have a negative connotation to it, implying we need to fix something that's wrong. Living our best and happiest life is to let our beautiful qualities shine through. I would no longer set resolutions. Instead, I would create New Year's intentions.

With "The Year of Ang" afoot, I couldn't wait to apply my New Year's intentions. Something inside of me was shifting towards a new me—ready to live the happy life I deserved.

SET INTENTIONS

Creating an intention directs your vision of how you want the new year to unfold. It brings hope and possibility, not the resolve of fixing the inadequacies you think you have. Behind each thought is energy and, by using positive intention, you begin an energy flow surrounding your entire being. The Law of Attraction states that like attracts like, so when you have these high-level, positive thoughts, more positive energy manifests itself.

By setting intentions, you create your own reality. You fuel yourself with goodness and invite your desires into your life, instead of what you don't want. New Year's resolutions are often broken in the first month, but intentions can be a commitment to do what makes you happy and propel you towards a positive way of thinking.

It's when you set intentions that you see your potential, allowing a superb version of yourself to unfold. Have conviction in your thoughts and feel good knowing the universe is working its fabulous magic to bring you there. Your intention brings forth your reality, so align your thoughts and words to how you want to design your life.

CALL TO ACTION

What is it you want to create in the new year or even right now? Follow this reverse resolution formula to bring amazing energy into your life.

Choose an intention that brings positivity and happiness into your life. Be clear with it. Let there be no grey area or room for interpretation.

Write it down. Share it. Talk about it. Be accountable for what you want to achieve.

Do things often that reaffirm your commitment to your intention. Be consistent. Take actions that align you with your intention.

Give yourself props for having the capacity to want to set an intention.

LIFE LESSON TWENTY-FOUR: WORK YOUR INNER DIVA

"Always act like you're wearing an invisible crown."
—Author Unknown

*O*n January 1st, the epic "Year of Ang" was underway. Much like every other morning during my travels, I woke up with a smile on my face and a whimsical song of joy in my head. That particular morning, the tune I'd soon be introduced to was Beyoncé's latest release at the time, *Single Ladies*. Having not watched much TV since leaving home, I was unaware of its brilliant music video. My life was about to change.

Laura and I prepared a satisfying breakfast of scrambled eggs, wheat toast, and avocado, and settled in to enjoy our meal and watch TV. I took charge of the remote control and aimlessly flipped through channels. You know how there are certain moments in history when you remember exactly what you were doing and how you felt when you heard the news? This was one of those poignant moments for me.

I ended my channel-surfing on the Australian music channel when my eyes locked on Beyoncé's captivating presence. I was absolutely mesmerized. The black and white *Single Ladies* music video is so simple, yet so spectacular. The music video is just Beyoncé and two back-up dancers wearing plain black body suits, while performing a fabulous dance routine. It's understated, yet somehow you can't take your eyes off of it. I insisted that we watch it on repeat the entire day.

I took some time to explain to Laura the importance of Beyoncé's distant mentorship in my life. Since she released her first single with her group, Destiny's Child, in the late 1990s, she has cultivated a persona of strength and female empowerment that has changed the cultural landscape—all while projecting an air of class and beauty. She's redefined the word, "diva." Instead of having a high-maintenance, negative connotation, a diva equates to commanding positive attention, having confidence, and being 100 percent comfortable with her choices. Beyoncé's alter ego, Sasha Fierce, intrigued me by how deep she could tap into her self-assurance. That character was someone I strived to be, especially during my awkward teenage years.

In high school, I took several actions to follow in her footsteps, which included: visiting the tanning salon every day to emulate her glow; occasionally wearing a fuzzy cowboy hat inspired by the *Bugaboo* music video; speaking with a slight southern drawl; and blasting Destiny's Child from the factory-grade speakers in my mom's white, four-door Chevy Cavalier (otherwise known as my "bassmobile"). I even walked with a sexy swagger (which, in retrospect, may have looked like I had a bum knee). I felt I was my high school's answer to Beyoncé.

As Laura and I prepared to head out to the club that evening, I made it my goal to tap into my inner Beyoncé and learn the *Single Ladies* choreography top to bottom. If the song came on at the club, I'd impress and inspire others to dance with me—and I hoped they too would recognize their inner diva.

To create our dance practice space, we moved an armchair and a coffee table to ensure ample room. Frame-by-frame, Laura and I broke down the routine.

This entire scene brought me back to the late 1990s when my next-door neighbour, Reggie, and I would lock ourselves in my basement and, in preparation for school functions, learn dance routines made popular by the Backstreet Boys. We met daily after school and took the endeavor seriously. The long hours of practice proved to be worth it when Reggie and I took to the dance floor at the school dance and a circle formed around us. We won the crowd with our epic dance renditions to songs such as, *Backstreet's Back*, and Britney Spears' *Baby One More Time*. We infused passion into each hitch kick, barrel turn, and dance move. We channeled our inner divas.

After two to three hours of practice, Laura and I felt confident we had nailed the *Single Ladies* dance and were ready to perform publicly. We swished back one more glass of sparkling wine for good measure and headed out to the club. It was as though my high school glory days had returned full circle. Not too soon after, my moment to shine presented itself.

The undeniable beat of *Single Ladies* slowly mixed with the previous song, prompting us to make our way to the dance floor. Perhaps it was that last glass of sparkling wine that helped me delve a little deeper into the moment, but as we broke out the routine, we couldn't help but laugh. It didn't matter how silly we may have looked because at that moment, we owned our three square ft. of space and loved life. We connected to our inner divas.

WORK YOUR INNER DIVA

When I think of the word diva, I picture a woman standing tall and proud, unabashedly commanding the attention of any room. A diva is someone who holds no qualms about pursuing and achieving her dreams. A diva doesn't care what other people think. Being a diva begs the question, *What Would Beyoncé Do?*

Before I decided to travel and when I lost my job, all my insecurities bubbled to the surface. I questioned my abilities and my self-worth. Somehow though, from those low moments, I managed to tap into my inner diva and find clarity in moving forward. I decided to take on the world (quite literally), and booked a one-way ticket to

Thailand. When I found my inner diva (my inner Beyoncé), I knew I could conquer anything I set my mind to.

Some women, including myself, have an inherent need for betterment. While it's important to challenge yourself, step outside of your comfort zone, and strive to be your best, your need for improvement can be destructive to your self-esteem. Self-perception and reality can become disconnected, which I have seen result in low self-esteem for some of the most fabulous people I know.

We tend to create a script in our heads in moments of despair and think, *I'm not good enough* or *I'm not pretty enough.* These feelings of worthlessness can manifest in multiple ways. Sometimes though, when faced with your lowest moment, something magical happens. A light shines on you and the only direction to go is up. You discover fire and passion within you.

One of the original divas, Patti LaBelle, once said, "Being a diva means being your best." The fabulous Miss LaBelle, Beyoncé, and anyone else who works their inner diva, doesn't feel the need to lower or shrink down in their self-worth. When you tap into this inner strength, you have the power to rise above limiting thoughts and move forward with power and a little pizzazz.

CALL TO ACTION

To connect with your inner diva, you must recognize how fantastic you are. Here's how:

> ***Identify one aspect about yourself you really love.*** It can be your ability to paint, your awesome hair, or your cooking skills. It can be a tiny talent, a hobby, or something you're proud of.

> ***Play it up!*** Focus your time and attention on that aspect. (For me, while in Australia, it was dancing.)

Release harmful self-talk and replace it with strength and power. When in doubt, tell yourself, "Damn right, I'm fabulous!"

LIFE LESSON TWENTY-FIVE: JUST BREATHE

"If I just breathe, let it fill the space between, I'll know everything is alright."
–Michelle Branch

After deeming my diva night-out a success, I decided it was time to plan a trip to another country—well in advance this time. I sauntered over to the nearest travel agency (whose sole purpose was a travel agency—a far cry from the business model in Thailand) with only two criteria: to travel somewhere hot and exotic. Sydney serves as a major travel hub in the South Pacific, so I had a number of diva-worthy tropical travel destinations to choose from.

After sifting through marketing pamphlets and remembering my fondness of the book *Eat, Pray, Love*, I decided that my next venture must be Bali. My new friend Mitra, who I'd spent Christmas with, decided to join me. Sure, we'd only known each other for two weeks, but we felt that was ample time to get acquainted and take a trip together. Why the heck not? The minute my travel agent handed over my flight itinerary, I immediately felt butterflies of excitement.

With my trip to Bali booked, it struck me that I only had a few weeks left in Australia. I was quite comfortable with my Sydney routine and spending time with my friends. I knew, though, that I needed to once again embrace Travel Ang by exploring and creating new adventures.

Following a recommendation from Laura, I registered for a "hop on, hop off" bus tour up the eastern coast of Australia that allowed me to travel at my own pace and have plenty of accommodation options. If I reached a destination where I felt the vibe, I could stay however long I wanted and check in with the ever-rotating bus schedule. This "go with the flow" philosophy aligned with being Dramatically Zen.

Little did I know that, for the first time during my trip, I was about to face a true backpacker locale: a hostel.

My coastal adventure started off on the wrong foot when my Cadillac of backpacks mysteriously broke, causing me to cradle it like a 25 lb misshapen baby. I don't know when or how it happened, but I assumed it spontaneously self-destructed as a ploy to encourage drama.

Truth-be-told, other than the terrifying night camping in Thailand, I hadn't exactly roughed it. In Thailand, I stayed at my aunt's apartment or in private and beautiful guesthouses. In Australia, I stayed with friends. Now that I was heading off on my own, I needed to prepare and adapt to new, potentially uncomfortable accommodations. My friends had warned me that hostels would indeed take me outside my comfort zone. I'm not sure what I expected, but I hadn't mentally prepared myself for the reality of what was to come.

After the 10-hour bus ride from Sydney, I reached my first destination, "Surf Camp," also known on the map as "Spot X" or, in my recollection, Spot Anxiety. When I arrived at the hostel, I laid eyes on my sleeping accommodations: a tiny tin structure with four metal walls and two bunk beds. I laughed out loud and thought, *There has to be more than this, right? Right?!* I took five steps around the room, all that was required to have a complete tour, and realized that this was it. The minimalist decor and design was the standard for hostels.

Panic overwhelmed me and I wanted to scream-cry, but before I could sob uncontrollably, some friends I'd met on the bus invited me to participate in drinking games on the beach. The celebrations temporarily put my tears at bay, and my horror was diverted. With the consumption of copious amounts of cheap wine, I never fully dealt with my first introduction to a hostel, which would have made me very hostile. That night, thanks to the wine, I fell into a deep slumber nestled in a ball on the top bunk.

I woke at 6:00 a.m. the next morning with my worries a distant memory as I headed to my surf lesson. I felt the early-morning thrill of the ocean, channelling my inner Kate Bosworth in the movie *Blue Crush*, a classic and personal favourite. My level of innate coolness jumped by 15 points as I mounted the long-board, wearing my one-piece wetsuit. Surfing came somewhat naturally to me, as I was able to connect to the yogi mind/body/soul relationship I'd strengthened at Spa Samui. By incorporating the controlled breath practiced in yoga and meditation, I was able to keep my balance despite the unpredictable waves.

It took a few attempts to get a system going, though. At first, I kept self-sabotaging because I'd shake with excitement as soon as I stood up on the board. This resulted in several face-plants in the water (not fun). Once I was able to connect with my breath and focus on it, everything else came easily. I was riding the waves in Australia in January. I was loving life!

After graduating from surf school, the bus took us to my next destination, Byron Bay. For some reason unbeknownst to me, the bus dropped us off half a mile from our hostel, so it was literally a mad dash to secure a room. It was summertime and peak season, so tourists flocked to the beach town. Throngs of people walked up and down the main strip, and a palpable buzz of exciting energy was in the air.

At Surf Camp, I'd met two British girls and we made plans to be roomies. While they waited in the monstrosity of a line to book a room (Ang Urquhart does not wait in lines), I went to the ATM to withdraw money. Much to my shock and horror, my bank card refused to work. I'd drained my remaining cash to pay for the bus tour and desperately needed more funds to pay for the Byron Bay hostel. I took it in stride and told myself it was going to be okay once I went online and sorted it all out.

As I walked back to the hostel after attempting to put my financial stress out of my mind, I realized I was a little anxious. I don't know if it was a delayed hangover from the drinking games the night before, or if I was simply antsy. I just knew something was off.

When I returned to the hostel, the girls greeted me in the lobby with a sympathetic look of concern. My heart beat faster as they unleashed awful news on me. Due to the high occupancy, the three of us wouldn't be able to bunk together. Instead, I would have to bunk with three random strangers in a room smaller than the one at Surf Camp (and likely a million degrees hotter).

A tightness built in my chest as my mind struggled to accept the situation. I did not want to stay in that hostel. I hated this. My face became hot, my breath shortened and sped up, and anxiety engulfed me. With my frustration brewing, independent of any self-control, I began to cry. In front of everyone.

Much like back at the airport in Thailand when I lost my luggage, when faced with a highly stressful situation, I fall to tears, which makes the situation worse than it actually is. Throughout my travels though, I'd been able to tap into a heightened state of awareness and adopt a perspective change and re-evaluate what was happening around me. I needed to take a minute and just breathe.

In that moment at the hostel, I paused and slowly back-stepped out of the lobby. I needed "me time" away from the situation to come back to myself. I found a quiet spot in a nearby garden, closed my eyes and slowed my breathing. I needed to breathe and rise above my current state of anxiety to reach the calm, cool, and collected part of me. By composing myself, I detached myself from my negative emotions.

When I get overly emotional and hyper, my mental clarity ceases to exist and I become an embarrassing version of myself. My mind gets scattered, and I'm unable to think about any positive outcomes.

By drawing my attention inward and directing my focus on the rhythm of my breath, I point my troubled thoughts to a calmer and more peaceful place. Through continued breath, I'm released from the initial anxious hold and slowly feel better.

Although my immediate response to the hostel labeled me as "the crying girl" for the rest of my time in Byron Bay, in the end I was able to get myself out of my funk and move forward.

JUST BREATHE

When you get worked up, your breath shortens, which can begin the cycle of anxiety. This stressful type of shallow breathing, activated by your "fight or flight" system, is an evolutionary adaptation to keep you from harm. When you're in an anxious situation, your body reacts like it would in times of danger, and then chaos results. Even if there's no real threat, anxiety clouds your emotional guidance system with worried thoughts. By stepping back and concentrating on your breath, you connect your body and your mind, and reflect, not react.

Instead of focusing on external struggles, sit back and breathe, drawing your awareness inward. Concentrating on your inhalation and exhalation creates a more relaxed rhythm to the body. By slowing down, you're able to become mindful and consider your thoughts, feelings and actions more carefully. What you may have originally considered to be urgent can be viewed rationally and from a clearer perspective.

CALL TO ACTION

The great actress and comedian, Lily Tomlin, once said, "For fast-acting relief, try slowing down." If you feel stressed or anxious and want to feel better, take the time to slow down and connect with your breath.

Focus on your inhalation and exhalation. As you draw out each breath, notice how it soothes you and decreases your heart rate.

Take plenty of time to get into the groove of relaxing breathing. A general rule of thumb would be to count to 10, but take it further to 20 or even 30 seconds. Breathe however many breaths it takes to get into a peaceful state where your heart no longer flutters with anxiety.

Acknowledge with gratitude that you were able to take a step back and connect with your breath.

LIFE LESSON TWENTY-SIX: DO SOMETHING THAT SCARES YOU

"Ah but a man's reach should exceed his grasp, or what's Heaven for?"
—Robert Browning

After being labelled "the crying girl" in Byron Bay, it was necessary to redeem myself big time. Even though I hadn't been at my best, I'd still made new mates. One of them, Katie (also British, hence the return of my accent), had researched activities to participate in around Byron Bay. After visiting the nearby travel agency, she returned to the hostel with a mischievous smile on her face. She then presented her activity of choice, which went hand-in-hand with my coolness redemption opportunity: Skydiving. Without considering my paralyzing fear of heights, I agreed to go. Travel Ang had reemerged.

Adventurous Travel Ang was fueled by one of the major motivations for my travels: to have an open mind and therefore challenge myself. I wanted to channel inner strength and confidence, and look fear in the face. When confronted with new obstacles, I'd ignore any self-defeating thoughts and move forward with conviction and drama. Why not take that attitude of fearlessness to the maximum and jump out of a plane? Could there be anything more dramatic?

And then my rational mind took over. *Wait a minute—skydiving? I always wear a seatbelt. I wear a life jacket while boating at the cottage. I look both ways before I cross the street. I do things to ensure safety and that I stay alive. So why did I consider doing something that risked my life?* This was quite the paradox. All of my baser instincts suggested that I not go through with it. Perhaps it was because of that reason skydiving was so desirable to me.

I was committed to feeling self-love and healing, and decided this would be the perfect approach to continuing my journey.

On the day of the jump, I was anxious to get the madness over with before I changed my mind. Due to extreme wind conditions and a stubborn lingering cloud, we had to wait three excruciatingly long hours before we could jump. This gave me more time to think and consequently more time to question what I was about to embark on. My mind kept defaulting to a worst-case scenario where the parachute couldn't open and I'd cut through the air at top speed, plunging to my death.

I could back out now and maybe they'd even refund my fees, I thought while pacing back and forth. But then, a wave of clarity and strength took over. No, I was not about to back out. I dismissed all excuses and convinced myself I was not going to die that day. Travel Ang had arrived and was ready to conquer the skies of Byron Bay!

With this fierceness, I claimed my motto, "Go big or go home," and chose to jump the highest skydive in Australia. Because at this point, why not? Soon, I'd jump out of a tiny plane from 14,000 ft. in the air.

Finally, we were directed to suit up in our skydiving gear and board the plane. This was it. Prior to the jump, I'd been surprisingly calm. I was strapped to a dreamy Australian skydive instructor who assured me I was fine (which I took as a compliment to my looks rather than an assurance of my emotional state). That calmness dissipated as soon as the pilot made the announcement that we'd reached our target altitude and were ready to prepare for the jumps.

The first jumper geared up, ready to take the plunge. One moment he was sitting beside me, and the next he was gone—out of the plane and rapidly falling to the earth. Oh my God, this was happening.

I was ready to pull the chute (pun completely intended), but there was no turning back. I'd told myself throughout this trip that I was a strong, brave woman, and damn right I was going to do this. After getting the thumbs-up from my skydive instructor indicating we were next to jump, I braced myself, said a quick, silent prayer, and made my way to the open door.

Before I knew it, I was in the midst of a 60-second freefall over the stunning shores of Byron Bay. With the wind pushing up against my face, my mouth was forced into a perfectly creepy smile as the earth drew closer. Slicing through the clouds, I felt a crisp moment of clarity and appreciation looking out at the turquoise waters on the horizon. What a view! I was skydiving in Australia. This was one of the coolest things anyone has ever done. Ever.

As my feet settled on the ground, I felt like I had landed on a wonderfully plump pillow. I did it! I jumped out of a plane and lived to tell about it! The adrenaline rush felt like nothing I'd ever encountered. My heart was racing, I couldn't stop laughing, and I was jumping up and down in a bizarre fusion of jumping jacks and Highland dancing. I wanted to go back up and do it again!

After connecting with an amazingly brave version of myself, I realized I'd conquered both the air and the land. Now, I needed to complete the trinity by conquering the sea. So, I signed myself up for my next adventure: a three day, three night sailing trip through the glorious Whitsunday Islands.

DO SOMETHING THAT SCARES YOU

Skydiving allowed me to face not only my fear of heights, but also touches on that natural fear of death. The acronym FEAR, "False Evidence Appearing Real," teeters more to the real end of the spectrum when it comes to skydiving. I physically put myself in a situation where if something went wrong, the end result could have been death. This life lesson is not about falling thousands of feet at high speed, harnessed only by a large piece of cloth and another person. It's about feeling the rush of adrenaline, excitement, and panic. It just so happens that skydiving was what pushed the boundaries of how far I could go. It served as a mode of catharsis.

When you drop your inhibitions and deviate from your normal behaviour, it becomes a form of healing. Sometimes you need to put the fear of death in your back pocket and take risks. The awareness of the impermanence of life serves as a motivator to keep you from becoming complacent. You raise the bar to your highest potential and you toughen mentally. The surge of energy from doing something scary will not only uplift you, but give you power.

CALL TO ACTION

You've let go of fear and stepped outside of your comfort zone. The bar has been raised a little higher, so increase it further and do something that scares you, terrifies you or brings you into risky territory.

Determine what this action or activity is for you. It could be moving to another country, starting the business you've always dreamed of, or ending a toxic relationship. It's scary. It could even be terrifying.

Take time to meditate and see where you can apply this life lesson. It may not be now or even three months from now, but keep this on the back burner. It will come in handy when that risk comes into play and a decision needs to be made. Sometimes, you have to just go for it. The greater risk is missing out on something that could change you for the better.

Do something unnerving, ridiculous, and unreasonable. Do something that shakes you to the core. It just might be the life lesson you need to give yourself more confidence and guide you to be your best.

LIFE LESSON TWENTY-SEVEN: BE KIND TO YOURSELF

"You have brains in your head. You have feet in your shoes. You can steer yourself in any direction you choose. You're on your own, and you know what you know. And you are the guy who'll decide where to go."
–Dr. Seuss

The day after my epic skydiving experience, I travelled to Airlie Beach—the boarding point for my three-day sailing trip. Since the sailing trip wasn't departing for a few days, I planned to clock some serious beach time until then. But, much to my dismay, the weather chose not to cooperate and I spent two rainy days waiting. I'll gladly take warm rain in Australia over the harsh, freezing temperatures of a Canadian winter any day, but it did throw a major wrench in my plans to hit the beach and surf. Even though the weather was a bit of a bummer, I was still excited for my upcoming sailing adventure.

Little did I know, I was about to embark on my worst nightmare.

Once the rain stopped, eager to explore the enchanting seascape of Eastern Australia, I happily boarded our sailboat, cleverly named *Spank Me* (which may or may not have been a determining factor in selecting it). To prepare, I had filled my backpack with an array of fruit to prevent scurvy while on board, since I thought it was a real risk. I couldn't wait to sun myself on the deck of a yacht similar to P. Diddy's, sipping sparkling wine and dancing to hip hop music. My outlook may have been misguided.

The exterior of the boat was nice. It was an old racing boat that had recently been refurbished. The look of the boat in the marketing pamphlet is what initially drew me in, but I shouldn't have trusted the photos. Mini life lesson: never judge a book (or a boat) by its cover. Nothing—and I mean absolutely nothing—had been done to improve the interior of the boat. Stepping onboard the boat changed my entire experience for the worse.

It began with the scent—rather, the stench—of the galley, which should have been labelled the "poop deck". The washroom, which doubled as the shower area, wasn't wide enough for me to put my hands on my hips and was to be shared by 28 passengers. This wasn't going to work for me.

Before we set sail, the hostess reeled off the rules and basic guidelines of *Spank Me*, beginning with a 60-second water rule. That's right, each person was allowed to run the water for only one minute per day. I'm sorry, but it takes a hell of a lot longer than that to even wet my beastly hair, let alone wash it.

Then, it got worse. She went on to reveal that we had to find a sleeping buddy to share a bed with. Pardon me? I was by myself and knew no one. With only five minutes on board, I hadn't applied Life Lesson Six: Talk to Strangers, so I hadn't made a friend to spoon with, as that was the only way to sleep on the teeny tiny beds. I frantically looked around as everyone else paired off. My unresolved childhood trauma of being picked last in gym class or a group resurfaced.

Thankfully, a nice girl from England was also on her own and offered to be my sleeping mate. Phew! I thought things were looking better- that was until we got ourselves acquainted with the boat and checked out the sleeping quarters. The beds, not even suitable for a jail cell, were situated in a dark, humid crevice of the boat, and the beds themselves were damp and somehow managed to reek of wet dog.

As an anxious sleeper, I require specific conditions to fall asleep: a door and window visible at all times; Feng Shui elements throughout the room for balance and harmony; a running fan for white noise; my face washed and moisturized; and my teeth brushed and flossed. None of those elements were present on *Spank Me*, and what was there horrified, saddened and repulsed me. Tears of frustration welled up as I teetered back into my crying girl role, a persona I thought I'd left in Byron Bay. I did not want to be on this boat.

As I packed up my belongings and fruit, the captain of *Spank Me* came to see me, sat me down, and launched into a pep talk about giving the boat a chance. I argued with him, highlighting all the reasons why I hated the boat, but he was persistent with his case. Reluctantly, I channelled Travel Ang, harnessed strength, and decided to stick it out. Besides, this trip did cost me a pretty penny, and I was trying to keep tabs on my spending so that I wouldn't go down in history as the world's worst backpacker.

We began to head out to sea, where the motion of sailing through the waves with the warm wind against my face calmed me down slightly. About 10 minutes into our expedition, the drinks flowed freely and everyone became fast friends. Another underlying theme of this trip happens to be getting to know one another through cocktails. They don't call them "sociables" for nothing!

All the joy and excitement soon became a distant memory at bedtime—when my true nightmare began. I'd thought camping in Thailand was bad, but that was nothing compared to sleeping on *Spank Me*. The level of humidity that engulfed the boat was similar to a Bikram hot yoga class. I tried to finagle my way to a spot on the bed, where my sleeping "buddy," a term I was then using very loosely, was in the deepest sleep possible. One level away from a coma, the girl was sprawled in a starfish position right in the middle of the bed. She didn't wake or even budge when I tried to push her to the side. Never had I seen such a sound sleeper. I furiously grabbed my pillow and decided to set up a makeshift bed on the deck of the boat.

I'll admit that this part of my sailing adventure was pretty spectacular. There was no light for miles except for the phosphorus that shone through the water and the glimmering stars blanketing the sky. I'd never seen so many shooting stars—it was mesmerizing! For about five minutes, I felt at peace in my surroundings and thankful to be experiencing that moment.

Sadly, the serenity didn't last long. At 5:00 a.m., I was abruptly woken up by the boat-crew mopping the deck. To this day, I still don't understand why they simply didn't wake me up and ask that I move instead of slopping dirty mop water in my face. All the discomfort I felt from my restless sleep, followed by using a hot, urine-soaked washroom to brush my teeth was just too much to handle. Dealing with that much discomfort and stress just to use the facilities doesn't equate to fun or a positive challenge to help anyone's personal growth.

I jumped out of a plane. I swam with sharks. I pushed myself and felt stronger and more confident because of the process. What I didn't need was to feel grossed out this badly. Travel Ang had done all she could to accommodate the grotesque conditions. This was just too much. So, I asked myself, *How can I show some self-compassion? What's the kindest thing I can do for myself right now?* I trusted my physical and emotional wisdom and made the decision to get off the boat.

I took the captain aside and this time the discussion rang to a different tune—the tune of me requesting a boat to pick me up and take me back to shore. I said goodbye to the friends I'd made on *Spank Me*, packed my bags, and waited eagerly for the other boat to save me. I reasoned that I was in a state of shock after my distressing experiences and therefore spoke to no one during the return to shore on the "rescue" boat. I lost myself in my thoughts and resumed what my sailing excursion should have been—me sunning on the deck of the boat, listening to P. Diddy.

If I had stayed on *Spank Me*, I would've spiraled further into a negative cycle of being grossed out. By leaving, I acknowledged the need to put my personal well-being before anything else. I felt a monumental sense of relief and knew I'd made the right decision.

I knew my limits and felt empowered by my decision to leave. Though I strived to be Dramatically Zen throughout my travels, being aboard that sailboat had no outlet for becoming Zen.

When I returned from my sailboat saga, I reverted to one of my other modes of transit: traveling by airplane. With the extra two days gifted to me after leaving the sailing excursion, I decided to explore the Great Barrier Reef. Our plane, a seaplane with water-landing capabilities, took us on an hour-long excursion to a pontoon in the middle of a coral reef, where we were greeted with sparkling wine and music. My entire experience came full circle. Once again, my Dramatically Zen self was loving life!

BE KIND TO YOURSELF

Emotional suffering is based on individual interpretation, and in my situation on the sailboat, I'd translated my discomfort to suffering. The worst version of myself came through when I wasn't being kind to myself. The best version, however, revealed itself when I left the boat. My decision brought me peace and I returned to the state of happiness I'd embraced throughout the trip.

Self-compassion is simply extending kindness to yourself when you're in a situation of suffering, pain, or experiencing shortcomings. Part of being human is to experience failure, so instead of ignoring it or getting angry, provide yourself with warmth. In no way does this make you weak. Rather, it allows you to act mindfully and balance all facets of a distressing experience. When you're able to recognize your emotional suffering and deliberately take action to comfort yourself, you generate feelings of love.

CALL TO ACTION

When faced with an emotionally or physically uncomfortable situation (similar to my miscalculated sailboat adventure overseas), take time to assess your level of well-being. Sometimes the greater power is the decision to walk away from the situation.

Give yourself the power to say no. Next time you're presented with a situation that challenges your values or doesn't serve you, allow yourself to have an out. You may say yes when asked to push your boundaries, like giving a speech at a wedding, going camping for the first time, or attending a networking event. When you feel a situation will take away from your experience, rather than allow you to grow, declining may be the right thing to do.

Sometimes you have to say no to that sixth wedding invitation of the year. Sometimes you have to say no when a colleague asks you to help them out *again*. And maybe you have to say no when you're so unsettled that the power of positive thinking and intention won't uplift the situation.

It's wonderful to embrace an open mind and a loving heart, but to honour yourself, say no to things that don't align with your emotional guidance system. There's power in saying no.

LIFE LESSON TWENTY-EIGHT: BE OF SERVICE

"The best way to find yourself is to lose yourself in the service of others."
–Mahatma Ghandi

With my sailboat saga behind me, my time in Australia had come to an end. Rather than saying goodbye to the country, I said, "See ya later." One day, I would return and embark on more Australian adventures. I didn't stress about the sights I hadn't been able to see. Instead, I was grateful for the experiences I had and how I was able to enjoy them at a leisurely pace.

My new friend, Mitra, who I'd gotten to know while staying with Laura, had agreed to join me on my trip to Bali. We had only known each other for a few weeks, but Mitra was a seasoned traveller who welcomed new experiences. She spent time living in Africa working for a non-governmental organization and had her share of Dramatically Zen experiences in the process, including brushes with malaria and rabies. We clicked instantly.

On the flight to Denpasar, Bali, we actively put ourselves in an indulgent mindset. We sipped sparkling wine and ate dark chocolate, all while expressing gratitude for our fabulous lives. As fate would have it, our flight attendant also promoted this fab philosophy and used his customer service skills to contribute to our merriment.

I love when you can tell someone truly enjoys their job. Their enthusiasm radiates and their positive attitude shines through their actions and words. It's contagious. It's like a big warm hug. This is exactly how I felt about our flight attendant. His aura was charged with a concentrated effort to make our flight more enjoyable. He was immediately likeable, and I immediately wanted to hug him.

In a way, he reminded me a bit of myself, with a diva presence and an almost theatrical approach to his actions. He didn't walk up and down the aisles, he sauntered. A genuine smile stretched across his face as he addressed each passenger by either "lovey" or "sweetie." He even used a bit of flair bartending as he poured juice and soft drinks. I couldn't take my eyes off of him. It was clear that providing quality service was his top priority.

At one point during the flight, as I sat and reflected on my life with a slight smile on my face, the attendant sidled his way around my seat, presented a closed fist, and slowly opened his hand to reveal a chocolate treat. I nearly screamed! The dramatic way he executed this stirred up fantastic excitement and happiness within me. It made me appreciate how small actions of kindness can improve what could otherwise be a routine experience and make it into something much more marvelous.

The flight attendant is the perfect example of someone who lives his life with positive intention, making a solid effort to brighten another person's day. It's clear that he feels love in his heart and chooses to extend that divine love to those around him. He could have just gone through the motions, offering a service to get from point A to B. Instead, he used his outgoing and upbeat personality to positively affect someone else.

In my wedding planner days, I took great pride in the service aspect of my job. When it comes to weddings, people are emotionally invested in every minute detail, from place-cards to the midnight buffet to centrepieces to receiving lines. What some perceive as a minor detail, others see as the opposite. As a wedding planner-extraordinaire, I had to assess people's level of emotional attachment to whatever obstacle had been presented and relieve their stress and concern about it.

Delivering the greatest customer service I could, I put each bride at ease. I created trust so she felt assured that her event was in the utmost care. In showing genuine interest for the bride's happiness, a bond was formed. By being of service, I made my clients feel good and as a result, I felt pretty damn good myself—a lovely form of karmic exchange.

As I arrived in Bali, I felt uplifted because of the service of another. The flight attendant's actions affected me in such a positive way that I've since preached the importance of being of service. I still feel the positive effects of this experience like it was yesterday. If given the opportunity, wouldn't you want to do the same for another?

BE OF SERVICE

This life lesson is the inversion of the previous lesson, "Be Kind to Your Server." Being of service is an integral part of the journey to live your best life because it allows you to enhance someone else's experience. When you're of service, you have the ability to positively influence another person. You hold the power to be kind to people. It doesn't need to be reciprocated. Your integrity shines through when you're of service, aligning your actions with your values and heart.

Even though you're serving someone else, your spirit is elevated. You bring meaning to your actions. If you're having a bad day, help someone by being of service. You'll feel significantly better. By being of service, you allow the light and love within you to extend outward, thus lighting up the world around you.

CALL TO ACTION

To be of service, you can extend simple actions, such as:

Holding the door for the person behind you;

Offering advice to someone while going through the ever-arduous decision of making a selection at Starbucks;

Assisting your colleague or friend with a project;

Going above and beyond your regular job tasks or duties;

Asking thoughtful questions;

Asking how you can help; or simply,

Being courteous in tiny interactions with others!

LIFE LESSON TWENTY-NINE: RECHARGE WITH A SELF-CARE ROUTINE

"Too much of a good thing can be wonderful!"
–Mae West

*O*ur flight from Sydney to Denpasar was one of the most pleasurable modes of transit I'd ever experienced (fit for a diva, if you will). Suspended in a state of indulgence, we used this as inspiration to set the tone for our time in Bali. Mitra and I collected our luggage and made our way into the tropical paradise that defines Bali. I breathed a sigh of appreciation at the exquisite surroundings. I hadn't even left the airport and I was already dazzled.

And then, to top it all off, *it* happened—my Dramatically Zen celebrity moment.

Amidst the frenzied airport terminal, my sight narrowed to a vision I'd always dreamt of—being greeted at the airport by a personal driver holding a sign with my name on it. Every time I've witnessed this at the airport I've wanted it to happen to me. The person named on the sign MUST be important or celeb-like in some way or other, which is what I admittedly strive for in life. Never had I anticipated my mini-dream would be fulfilled, and of all places, at the Denpasar International Airport.

But there it was—my name on a placard held stoically above the head of a tiny Balinese man. My dream had come true! I let out a high-pitched squeal of joy and clapped in a circle of delight (Ang Urquhart loves when people clap in a circle). Sure, the sign he made was my first name written in bubble letters on a sheet of lined paper, but it was perfect. As I celebrated my celebrity airport welcome, I led Mitra over to our greeter. Much like most of the first-born males in Bali, his name was Wayan.

The reception at the Denpasar Airport with Wayan was pre-arranged by my Spa Samui yoga teacher, Anna, in Thailand. She'd been visiting him and his family for years and was even helping them start up a bed and breakfast. I trusted Anna's recommendation, and reserved Wayan's services as a driver and host during our time in Ubud, the art and cultural centre of Bali. After quickly introducing ourselves to Wayan, we made our way to his vehicle and loaded up our belongings.

In a way that had become characteristic of my travels, I arrived with no plan for a place to stay or activities to experience. Mitra and I put our confidence in Wayan, asking him for recommendations. Based on his advice, we booked four nights at the Monkey Forest Road Bungalows, located on none other than Monkey Forest Road. (Best. Name. Ever.)

To get to our guesthouse, we made our way through a perfectly manicured Balinese garden. A small stone pathway led us to a cascading waterfall flowing into a large glistening emerald pond brimming with pearl and magenta water lilies. Lining the enclosed garden area, stone carvings in the shape of mystical Hindu gods framed the foliage, and exotic flowers were impeccably placed amidst the splendor of it all. We took our time wandering through the horticultural masterpiece, appreciating every vibrant colour of the flowers.

Upon our arrival at our guesthouse (which was nothing short of paradise), our eyes locked on the intricate details of the magnificent door that opened into our authentic Balinese quarters. Fresh flowers graced every corner of the room, which featured a teak hand-carved canopy bed adorned with genuine Batik linens. I'd never experienced a more romantic setting. What an introduction to the idyllic island! The next morning, we awoke to the sound of roosters and began our day by exploring Monkey Forest Road. We discovered that the forest at the end of the road housed a large population of Balinese macaques monkeys (hence the name). The monkey discovery was a reward in and of itself. We strolled up and down Monkey Forest Road, where every shop lining the street showcased the beautiful crafts, opulent fabrics, and ornate paintings and carvings that represent the Hindu culture.

The majority of the Indonesian population is Islamic, whereas the natives of Bali practice one of the most ancient forms of Hinduism. The religion first came to Indonesia several centuries ago by way of Indian traders, who travelled across the sea of Java from India. An eventual violent religious uprising occurred across the nation, forcing several members of the Indonesian royal family, who were devoted to their specific branch of Hinduism, to flee. They ended up on the island of Bali—not a bad place to land if I do say so myself!

With these elite individuals came their extended royal family members, their craftsmen, and their priests (basically, the crème de la crème of society). On that first morning in Bali, I could see that this was an island fit for royalty. This regal presence echoed throughout generations to present-day Bali where the locals are a combination of royalty, artists, and spiritual leaders. The fusion of the beauty of the Island and cultural pride can be seen through the hand-crafted masterpieces lining the streets, thus a creating sensory overload.

Life in Bali involves a continuous cycle of offerings and rituals. Every morning, the locals burn incense and give offerings to their many gods. The sweet fragrance of incense lingers in the air. The spiritual commitment displayed through elaborate hand-carved statues and harmonizing decor adds to the overall mystique.

In the spirit of the sacred Balinese rituals, Mitra and I decided to luxuriate in a ritual of our own: self-care. It was pure serendipity that Monkey Forest Road also happened to be lined with the most lavish collection of spas I'd ever seen. Every 10 ft. we were greeted with a new and even more glamorous spa offering. After careful consideration, we agreed on a spa retreat that included a full body massage, body scrub, yogurt body treatment, flower bath, and a facial—all for $15! Did I mention how much I was loving life?

Our afternoon of luxury left us feeling rejuvenated, relaxed, uplifted, and super clean. I had a hop in my step, and actually clicked my heels in the air a few times because it felt right. With an emotional, physical, and almost spiritual response to living in the lap of luxury, we proclaimed our Balinese travel mission: we would explore the spas of the Island. We gave ourselves permission to indulge in self-care—and I couldn't think of a better way to spend our evenings after sunning ourselves on the beach all day.

At this stage in my travels, indulging and treating myself allowed me to be further suspended in joy.

RECHARGE WITH A SELF-CARE ROUTINE

When you take time to indulge in self-care, your only objective is to feel good. By carving out time in a busy schedule, you pause external chatter and focus on nurturing yourself. You take time to recharge your batteries. We often put other people's needs in front of our own, even at the cost of our well-being and personal comfort.

I was fortunate enough to experience these luxuries for only about $10 per visit and am certainly aware of the cost difference for similar services in North America. Regardless of the cost, the investment in yourself is still worthwhile. Give yourself permission to indulge in an action that will boost your spirits and allow you to let go of any tension or worry you may have been holding onto. Treat yourself and create that promising light at the end of the tunnel—it will serve as a motivator in your weekly routine.

CALL TO ACTION

Go beyond having an occasional "You Day" and create a self-care routine. It can be as simple as setting boundaries between work and play or having a dedicated night in (or night out) once a week.

Identify your personal self-care practices. For example, get a massage, disconnect from social media and email, have a special meal, or curl up with a book you've been dying to read.

Express gratitude for indulging yourself. With the circle of indulgence complete, you'll feel recharged and ready to be the best and most awesome version of yourself.

LIFE LESSON THIRTY:
SPEND TIME IN NATURE

*"Climb the mountains and get their good tidings. Nature's peace
will flow into you as sunshine flows into trees. The winds will blow
their own freshness into you and the storms their energy, while cares
will drop off like autumn leaves."*
–John Muir

After a few days of living in the lap of luxury and indulgence, Mitra and I decided it was time to explore something other than the spas of Bali. We were whole-heartedly embracing self-care and enjoying ourselves immensely, but we wanted some physical activity to offset the lavish amount of relaxation.

With this intention, I called Wayan and asked if he would be willing to be our tour guide around Ubud, and show us the immaculate rice terraces that paint the landscape of Bali. Wayan, the ever-gracious host, offered to take us on a hike to his village. Little did we know, we were about to embark on an eight-mile trek through the dense rainforest of Bali.

Wayan picked us up at our guesthouse, where we leisurely strolled down Monkey Forest Road and found a path that led to a field of rice paddies. We carefully walked on a small shelf of earth cleared completely of trees above the flooded land. The intricate labyrinth was created for the sole purpose of growing rice. I was so overwhelmed by the artistic quality of it all that I failed to notice Wayan leading us into the thick Balinese jungle. While we did crave some physical activity, I'm positive Wayan thought we were in the market for gladiator-esque challenges.

We began our hike karate-chopping our way through an impenetrable forest where I suffered minor flesh wounds on my forearms, which Wayan found to be comical. It wasn't a smooth start, but the scenery kept my mind balanced in a positive place. About 20 minutes later, we were faced with the extreme challenge of scaling down a cliff wall with a deadly 90 degree angle drop. That was when things got very real, very quickly.

If faced with this sort of outdoor challenge in Canada, I would have prepared by purchasing proper hiking shoes and rock climbing gear. In this moment, however, I wore a strapless bathing suit top, Billabong short shorts, and Havaianas thong sandals. Needless to say, not appropriate jungle hiking wear.

I stared at the valley below, determining where and how to begin. Somehow the height felt more daunting than when I was about to skydive out of an airplane. One misstep and I would end up with a lot more than a flesh wound, and I wasn't sure how dependable my medical insurance was at that point. Wayan smiled and waved me over to the ravine, then easily climbed down in under two minutes.

Well, that looked easy enough! It was my turn. I took a deep breath in for control and a sharp exhale out for a mantra of confidence. I settled one foot in a small ridge of the cliff, tested my footing, felt secure, and continued down slowly, one foot at a time. Before I knew it, both feet were safely planted on the ground.

After repelling down the cliff with no actual repel, I took a moment to observe my surroundings. So focused on not tumbling to my death, I'd overlooked the amazing jungle scenery. I inhaled deeply and felt at the apex of being alive. I was in the middle of a jungle and felt humbled to be in the untouched rawness of nature.

When faced with our next challenge, I couldn't help but laugh. We were to cross a thin bamboo bridge suspended 80 ft. above a valley, which was strewn with jagged rocks. In a way, I felt like Baby in *Dirty Dancing* when she had to dance across the log over water (except Patrick Swayze wasn't on the other side waiting to greet me and Baby wasn't suspended high up with the threat of death looming should the bridge collapse).

Using my core muscles, I cautiously placed one foot in front of the other while mouthing a silent prayer of safety (something I'd realized I was doing often throughout my travels). I temporarily put my fear aside and breathed in. Much like yoga and meditation, I focused only on my inhalation and exhalation and made my way across the precariously swaying skeletal bridge.

With my feet safely on solid ground, I mindfully breathed in the glorious fresh air. I paused and gazed out at the tiers of intricate rice terraces that unfolded beneath me. I became enveloped in the natural state of life around me and with that, a sense of clarity took over. Although it took a few extreme outdoor challenges, my takeaway was quite clear at that moment: being surrounded by the jungle and immersed in nature made me feel rejuvenated and alive. During my travels, I'd enjoyed much of my time outdoors experiencing the beauty of our planet, but our trek reinforced the importance of spending time in nature.

With our hiking challenge completed, Wayan led us back onto the main road, which was 20 ft. away from us the entire time. Did we really need to take the dramatic jungle route to view the rice paddies and arrive at our final destination? No, we didn't (that sneaky Wayan)! If we hadn't taken the more difficult route though, I may not have had the opportunity to embrace the life lesson of spending time in nature, and because of that revelation, I was grateful.

SPEND TIME IN NATURE

Our lives tend to move in fast motion. Cars speed by with lights flashing red, yellow, and green. The signals and images on our computer screens strain our eyes and artificially stimulate the brain. Our mind runs at top speed to keep up with a fast-paced society. Stepping away and placing ourselves in nature's regenerating energy connects us to an organic state of life.

Spending time in nature calms the mind. A sensory awareness is created from the beauty of the earth's bounty. Whether it is rice paddies, trees, flowers, or trickling streams, surrounding yourself with nature provides an escape from the urban landscape you're exposed to day in and day out. Nature provides an outlet for peace and relaxation.

While immersed in nature, you're filled with stimuli that modestly ask for your attention. Your mind focuses on the ever-present subtleties of nature, providing relaxation and restoration. As an added bonus, your lungs fill with fresh air instead of toxic fumes and smog that can come with city life.

While it may be difficult to immerse yourself in nature every day, it's key to a healthy life balance. Studies have shown that spending time in nature allows for decreased feelings of depression, increased levels of self-esteem, and reduced stress. It brings happiness. Spending excessive amounts of time inside can make you feel sluggish, but when you step outside and breathe in the rejuvenating splendor of nature's gifts, you feel more alive.

CALL TO ACTION

Exercising and spending ample time outdoors will allow you to produce a trickle effect of positivity to your health and wellness.

Write yourself a prescription to "get green" and spend time in nature.

Try going for a bike ride, walk, run or swim; taking a hike; taking your yoga mat outside for a restorative yoga practice; joining a recreational sports team; strolling the beach;

reading outdoors in a lounge chair; or feeling the warmth of the sun or coolness of the wind on your face.

LIFE LESSON THIRTY-ONE: HAVE A TOTEM OF STRENGTH

"Life only demands from you the strength that you possess."
—Daj Hammarskjold

*M*y last day in Bali included the final massage of my trip, which added up to an astounding 11 massages in 12 days. After trekking through the Balinese jungle, I decided to fuse the life lessons of spending time in nature with self-care, so from that moment on, I requested to have my massages outdoors.

As my travels neared to an end, I reflected on my experiences with my "Bucket List of Love." The list was a work in progress, edited, re-edited, and adjusted harmoniously as different opportunities presented themselves. There was something, however, that remained constant: I wanted to get a tattoo. I'd been contemplating getting one since my arrival in Thailand but decided to wait because the excessive sun exposure would adversely affect it (and I didn't want to mess with my tanning potential so early in the trip). But in Bali, I had a perfectly bronzed tan, my skin was exfoliated to perfection from my spa experiences, and I would head home soon. All the stars aligned and I felt ready.

I hastily dove into other decisions throughout my trip without considering future consequences. By scuba diving, I could've been eaten by sharks. By skydiving, I could've face-planted into the earth. This tattoo, however, was something that had been in the back of my mind since my Nonno passed. I wanted to honour him through artwork etched on my body, so it would last forever. I also wanted to get it done in a special place, as it would represent one of the most special people in my life. Upon arriving in Bali, I knew the time had come.

I decided to get my Nonno's name, Rocco, tattooed on the back of my neck. (Replicating Posh Spice's tattoo may or may not have been a contributing factor in the placement). The name Rocco literally means rock, and he was exactly that. He was my rock, my strength, and my driving force throughout these past few months of travel. I knew my Nonno was watching over me and providing me with strength in whatever way guardian angels do. When I thought of him smiling down on me, and at times likely laughing at me, I was filled with happiness and personal power. I needed this strength to remain with me. A tattoo of his name would serve as a totem of strength, so when I reflected on it, I would feel strong. A lot was riding on this tattoo, so I mapped out the perfect (which also happened to be the only) tattoo parlour in Ubud.

Bali is located six degrees south of the equator. The tattoo parlour was lined with floor to ceiling windows that let in the hot afternoon sun. Palm trees and exotic plants framed the entrance, trapping the humidity and heat into the 12 sq. ft. room, or more appropriately, sauna. I was in the hottest place possible. The opportunity for bacteria was a high risk—but I'd already decided to go for it. The tattoo artist, who stood as tall as my hipbone, consulted his friend about the translation of "Rocco" into Bahasa Indonesia script, the language spoken in Bali. In retrospect, I have no idea why his friend was even there. Strange.

After about 25 minutes of sketching and re-sketching, he gave me a curious smile and the thumbs-up. Based on his difficulty with the translation, I deduced this might have been the first time he tried to translate such a word. I put my trust in him completely and believed that whatever he was tattooing on the back of my neck was indeed my Nonno's name and not "big, tall, weird, creepy girl" in script.

So with Mitra holding my sweaty hand, I proceeded with the tattoo (and reminded myself of Life Lesson Twenty-Five: Just Breathe). By applying my metaphorical totem of strength, I mustered up inherent strength and breathed through the pain. A short 10 minutes later, with results even more fantastic than I could have expected, I had a new tattoo.

From then on, I'd forever hold that symbolic image specific to me and only me. It'd remind me of the strength I'd been able to tap into during my travels—travels I knew my Nonno was watching over and protecting me throughout. He was the main reason I set out on my travels of healing and love. The beautiful Balinese letters cascading down the back of my neck were a representation of my strength Nonno would be proud of. It would become my reference point when I needed to draw on courage and personal power.

On that final day of paradise in Bali, I finally had a beautiful, meaningful tattoo. From that day onward, whenever I take a moment and reflect on it, I know with absolute conviction I have the capacity to conquer anything.

HAVE A TOTEM OF STRENGTH

As I left Bali, I realized the importance of finding a totem of strength. Your totem of strength can be something kept with you, whether it's an object, a tattoo, an image, or a symbolic representation. This item serves as a conductor for your emotions. Its intrinsic value is rooted with strength that lifts you up and reminds you of your personal power.

When drawing your attention to your totem, your focus shifts to the strength you placed behind it. In turn, this action can lessen the impact of heightened emotions or stress. It brings you to the here and now, instead of getting caught up in past worry. It grounds you and brings you back to the present. When you feel grounded, you feel in control. When you're in control, you can tap into your inherent strength and move forward.

When you feel yourself becoming unsettled or uneasy, refer back to your totem of strength and reflect on the meaning within it. In doing so, you'll know that whatever sadness or strain you feel will soon pass. Mindfully connecting to your object of strength also connects you to your inner strength. Your comfort and confidence levels will rise because you will be aware of the strength that naturally resides within you. This life lesson highlights just one of the ways to unite your present state to this personal power, elevating you to happiness.

CALL TO ACTION

Find your own totem of strength. This is personal to you. Some examples are a special stone, a piece of jewelry, a photograph, or even a written message.

Hold onto your totem and transfer positive thoughts to it. As a mind exercise, send strength into this object and infuse it with meaning.

Whenever you need to draw strength, come back to your totem and know that it's there for you. If you feel sad, hold onto your object, close your eyes, and use this exercise as a grounding tool. Your strength is there, and your totem will help you draw it out again.

LIFE LESSON THIRTY-TWO: PRACTICE PATIENCE

"Patience serves as a protection against wrongs as clothes do against cold. For if you put on more clothes as the cold increases, it will have no power to hurt you. So in like manner you must grow in patience when you meet with great wrongs, and they will then be powerless to vex your mind."

—Leonardo Da Vinci

My journey of healing and love was coming to an end. After three months, three countries and thousands of Dramatically Zen memories, I was prepared for the next chapter, armed with all I'd learned. First though, I had to endure the flight home.

They say, "patience is a virtue," but I doubt whoever came up with that proverb ever had to endure a 30-hour flight overseas.

Unless you are flying first class, you can't possibly enjoy a long flight (and especially one that takes a day and a half to arrive at your final destination). I couldn't overcome the dread, and anxiety soon followed. I just wanted to get home. The nearly 30-hour flight included three layovers, so I had no choice but to become versed in patience.

It was 4:00 a.m. on a Tuesday in February when I arrived at the airport (Ang Urquhart does not like early mornings). All I wanted to do was check my backpack, which by that point was painfully heavy with all my souvenirs. I clumsily dragged the luggage behind me as it morphed into the now morbidly obese baby. Not an ideal situation.

To add to my frustration, the airline attendant instructed me multiple times to change queues. ("Queue" sounds much more elegant and British than "line"). Each queue I moved to seemed to end up being longer than the previous one. She clearly didn't understand the universal truth that Ang Urquhart does not wait in queues. I wasn't sure what was going on other than this woman found humour in my confusion and struggles with my luggage. With the constant queue-changing, my wait time doubled. This was the first instance I had to tap into the moral high ground of patience, and not scream, which was exactly what was going on in my head.

By applying a combination of patience and Life Lesson Twenty-Five: Just Breathe, I held back the impulse of releasing my frustrations and became centred, controlled, and calm. I instantly felt more peaceful and was even able to see the hilarity of this Balinese version of "musical chairs"—with multiple airport queues instead of chairs.

I applied the second dose of patience when I finally boarded the plane and prepared for the first of three flights home. How fantastic would it be if every flight were a direct one? I approached the row my assigned seat was in and let out a long, dramatic sigh (similar to one my Nonno would have released), as I realized that I'd be stuck for the next seven hours in a middle seat. Following my sigh of despair, I breathed in a cleansing breath of light, love, and patience to once again become centred (tapping into Life Lesson Fifteen: Meditate). I decided to view this annoying situation through loving eyes and attempted to get comfortable.

Because the universe loves to test me, a woman with a tiny, rambunctious toddler settled into the seat directly in front of me. Oddly, the child kept staring and making creepy eye contact with me. I tried to use my open mind and loving heart mantra (and a touch of Life Lesson Six: Talk to Strangers) and entertain this adorable child. With a goofy grin on my face, I launched into a modified dance-version of peek-a-boo, which in my opinion was genius. The child, however, was not amused and immediately burst into tears. This continued on and off for the next seven hours.

While I cringed again, I had to accept that this situation was happening, regardless of my positive or negative thoughts. I needed a different and more tolerant perspective. By conjuring up patience, using noise-canceling earphones, and tapping into Life Lesson Twelve: Listen to Music, I became centred and found there was no need for me to feel anxious. This was all part of the process of getting home. Instead of worrying about what the next day would bring, I decided to contend with the present.

Patience takes endurance and a clear mind, which contributes to a clear and rational outlook. What better place to practice the art of patience than on a flight to the other side of the world?

After 30 long hours of flight, I made it back to a snowy, blustery Toronto. The enormous amount of patience I'd exercised during the agonizingly long journey, coupled with my inability to sleep on planes, heightened my anticipation to collapse onto my own bed. I'd only clocked approximately two hours of sleep, with the help of wine, of course. When I arrived at the airport, I was staggeringly delirious.

Rocking a kick-ass tan that would rival that of my grandparents circa Acapulco 1987, I sauntered my way over to the luggage carousel to gather my belongings. I waited and waited. Slowly, a familiar feeling of panic came over me. My backpack was nowhere in sight.

Rather than falling to tears (my default), I took a deep breath and rationally considered what could have happened. Patiently, calmly, and with a slight British accent, I explained to the Air Canada agent that my beloved backpack was missing. I think she was applying Life Lesson Twenty-Nine as she displayed the most wonderful customer service and within minutes, found my bag. It was on the other side of the country in Vancouver. Oh, come on! Apparently, after I boarded my second connecting flight in Japan, there had been an announcement instructing passengers to retrieve and re-check their bags for the final flight home. During the announcement, I'd been practicing patience, as well as cracking a bottle of wine, and therefore failed to pay attention. I'd have to apply a final bout of patience since it would be a few more days until my bag would arrive and be delivered to my house.

Yes, it was true I wanted to immediately rip open my luggage and wear all 36 scarves I'd purchased in Thailand and Bali, but I'd have to wait. I had no choice but to explore one of patience's counterparts: delayed gratification. In applying the loving stance of patience (now a familiar friend), I self-regulated and adapted my mindset to overcome the demands of the environment. I'd appreciate my scarves even more when I received them a few days later.

Let's be honest. I wouldn't be Dramatically Zen if my travels ended smoothly and without a hitch. You know what Universe? Bring on the drama!

PRACTICE PATIENCE

Sir George Savile, the English politician, once wrote, "A man who is a master of patience is a master of everything else." Translate that to modern day. A woman who can wait for 36 silk scarves from Thailand is a woman with self-control. Sometimes you're presented with situations or circumstances that aren't ideal, which affects your emotional state. Your reactions can teeter towards impatience, stress, and annoyance. You have the ability to make the situation worse by responding negatively. On the other hand, you have the opportunity to react in a cool, calm, and patient way, rising above the stress. Your personal power and strength of character lies within your response to situations like these. Practicing patience will allow you to tap into your power, take control, and rise above to reach happiness.

If you learn to harness your anxiety about the outcome of a goal or destination, you can truly begin to look at the situation from a calm and relaxed point of view. The nagging frustration of impatience only serves to bring on a disheartened mindset. Instead of appreciating the present, you worry about the future and negate to see the beauty in the present moment.

CALL TO ACTION

How do you find patience when you feel engulfed in discomfort, anxiety or irritability?

First, acknowledge that patience is needed, which will allow you to tap into your capacity to tolerate an uncomfortable or stressful situation.

Next, do something that grounds you and calms you down. This could be applying a variety of other life lessons, such as, breathing, meditating, or finding your totem of strength. Draw your attention to the present instead of the future.

Finally, let go of your anxious hold. Time isn't going to move faster if you let stress get the better of you. Once you are able to let go, you will find peace in practicing patience when it's needed most.

LIFE LESSON THIRTY-THREE: DECIDE, TAKE ACTION, AND ALLOW

"Twenty years from now you will be more disappointed by the things that you didn't do than by the ones you did do. So throw off the bowlines. Sail away from the safe harbor. Catch the trade winds in your sails. Explore. Dream. Discover."

–Mark Twain

On my first day back in Canada, I felt nostalgic and found myself deep in thought about the previous few months. My backpack had been returned earlier that morning, and I felt at peace. As I sat in my living room, wrapped in a blanket and four silk scarves, I thoughtfully and dramatically gazed out the window (Beyoncé music playing in the background). While enjoying some "me time," I reflected on my experiences abroad and concluded that, much to my friends' disbelief, the following hadn't happened:

1. I did not convert to Buddhism and/or Hinduism.

2. I did not contract rabies.

3. I did not have to sell my sleeping pills for money.

4. I did not get married.

5. I did not get arrested for illegally downloading episodes of *The Office*.

6. I did not get my hair braided into cornrows.

7. I did not join a hill tribe in northern Thailand.

8. I did not come back with an accent (debatable).

9. I did not switch my flight to come home at a later date.

Although I kind of wish I'd joined a hill tribe in northern Thailand for bragging rights, what I did come home with stretched far beyond any expectations I'd had. Life was different. I was different. I was happy! This happiness wasn't a fleeting wave of emotion that would ebb and flow as the days went by. It was a sustained happiness that felt boundless. My heart was whole and full. The best life I was seeking out to live was actually happening!

And now, it was my duty to continue onward with my dreams. This was my divine purpose. Even though I'd never done it before and I wasn't sure where to start, I was going to write the book I'd set out to write prior to my trip. The material was there. I just had to transform that into my own art.

So, I began.

I logged onto my computer and for the first time, took a few hours to read over my blog entries from the past few months—from my first hectic entry about packing to my last entry before I boarded the plane home. I was mystified. Did I really do all of that? It felt as though I was reading an inspirational story about someone else's life I couldn't turn away from. A smile formed over my face. This was MY inspirational story!

In creating my own story, I used inspired action. Inspired action is rooted in positive feelings and when taking the necessary steps, my entire being consistently radiated joy. My intuitive nature was ignited and I felt empowered. Inspired action creates even more inspired action. Before I knew it, I found more inspiration in the events around me, and they were events I could easily write about.

Publishing my travel blog online created more momentum. People actually cared about what I wrote and tuned in daily to read my posts. I included a count-metre on my website, so the interest in my writing could be quantified. Day after day, I received hundreds of hits on my blog. I was astonished at how the number of website visits went from 100 hits one day to 1000 hits by the week's end. As I sat down at my computer and reviewed the activity around my blog, the magnitude of its impact sank in.

I read through the comments section and felt overwhelmed by the positive messages. The feedback I received from friends, acquaintances, and even random readers who stumbled across my blog in a Google-search, fueled me with positivity and reinforced I was on the right path. These extrinsic motivators contributed to the pursuit of my intrinsic power, my inner joy. It pushed me even further to take action by continuing to write.

When I look back on my experiences in publishing my blog, I'm able to say I loved every moment of what I was doing. I loved the emotions my travels stirred up within me. I loved sitting down and writing in my journal, and translating my journal points into a blog post. Now, here I was reviewing all of these inspired actions and adapting it into a book. The goal I set out to achieve was coming to fruition. Holy crap! This was exciting!

CALL TO ACTION

I viewed my trip as perfectly successful. The ups and downs, bouts of crying, and of course, moments of inspiration and clarity were all contributing factors. I attributed my success to achieving personal fulfillment and applying simple life lessons to get there.

I accomplished what I set out to do, and I believe you can do the same once you figure out what YOU want to achieve. I thought long and hard about how I reached this exhilarating point. I followed these three distinct steps to transition from where I was to where I needed to be. It's my absolute pleasure to share them with you:

1. DECIDE

One axiom of success states, "The universe rewards action." By going on my trip, I took the necessary steps to become someone who made decisions to move forward. I've learned that the universe has a magical and powerful ability to hone in on the wondrous combination of desire and action. It serves as a magnet to attract other events, people, and circumstances that contribute to lofty goals. All I had to do was decide what I wanted and give it my full attention. I decided to travel, write, and follow my dreams.

2. TAKE ACTION

When I booked my ticket to Thailand, a flame ignited within me. I had absolutely no idea how my trip would pan out or what adventures it would bring. I only knew I was inspired and, in following the positive mindset of having an open mind and loving heart, the universe revealed many experiences that have forever changed me.

In having my actions revolve around my dreams and goals, it felt like there was a warm loving light radiating from my body. This is what it feels like when your whole body smiles. To be able to say, "I am living my dream," reaffirms my belief that you truly can achieve anything. I'm a prime example of someone who took action to pursue her dream. Action is how we achieve success. Action results in inspiration.

3. ALLOW

Connecting with the best version of myself has allowed me to trust my actions. By trusting myself, I was brought to a position where all the planning and analyzing was released, and faith in my decisions was restored. There was no back-peddling, regret or second-guessing. What remained was a deep trust and faith that everything would work out for the best.

And everything truly did work out in one dramatic way or another. I was inspired to travel to Thailand and beyond, and my trust enabled me to follow my dreams and live the journey of a lifetime. I had to be open and allow everything lingering overhead to culminate into all those moments of joy.

Sometimes you need to get out of your own way and try. You never regret actions taken, but you will always feel the pang of regret if you don't try. You won't regret giving your dreams a chance. And when you decide to follow your dream, your life will change immediately. Trust me. I tried, and I was rewarded a million times over. If I could do it, you can too!

~ ~

Life is an absolute masterpiece with the purpose of creating events, experiences, and goals to teach us lessons, and ultimately, bring us joy. What benefit is there in living a life without excitement? Why aren't we continually on a journey to happiness?

Happiness is a choice, and we all possess endless potential to cultivate it. There are limitless possibilities as to where our imagination and capabilities can take us. First, we must decide what we want to create in our lives. Next, we need to take actionable steps towards that goal, whether they're bold actions like booking a plane ticket or smaller actions like reading a motivational book. The key is to take action forward. And finally, we must allow the good to happen by being receptive to the magic that the universe holds.

What prevents us from allowing ourselves to become the best version of the person we're meant to be? What stops us from living up to our full potential? Fearlessly ask yourself, "What is preventing me from taking action?"

Identify what has caused you to hold back. It could be one of the roots of a life lesson presented in this book: fear, issues with self-esteem, or unhappiness. It could be focusing on past mistakes that inhibit you from facing new challenges, or that you just don't know how to take action to move forward. It could be that you're waiting for the perfect moment when all the stars align.

I am here to tell you that that moment is NOW.

I created a dream for myself and decided I wasn't going to let anyone or anything stand in the way of my personal ambition. I set it, sought it and, because the universe is kind and I am kind to it, I achieved it. I travelled, I found the best version of myself, I wrote about my adventures and, if you are reading this right now, well hell, I published my book!

When I look back at where I was to where I am now, I become giddy with happiness. I am in this place because I took action, created my own life-defining moments and refused to settle for anything less than my Dramatically Zen dream.

I stepped away from my computer and reassumed my cozy position on the couch, notepad and fancy pen in hand. At the top of a fresh page, I wrote "Dramatically Zen." I was about to enter a new and even more creative phase in my life, and those 15 letters were the beginning.

Somewhere in heaven, my Nonno, my rock, is smiling down on me. He is my driving force and strength, and I'm certain he's proud that I'm living, and will continue to live, the best version of myself. He's proud I'm living my dream.

"The real voyage of discovery consists not in seeking new landscapes,
but in having new eyes."
—Marcel Proust

ABOUT THE AUTHOR

$\mathcal{N}$othing brings me greater joy than seeing people follow their dreams—taking risks for the sake of happiness, aiming for that previously "unreachable" goal, or even setting out on that travel adventure that has been brewing for years.

Something magical happens the moment people let go of their self-limiting beliefs and start following their passions and their heart. A new and stunning energy surrounds them and they glow.

When I took off on my journey overseas, I finally ignited that gorgeous glow.

Since then, I haven't stopped aiming for greatness and striving to be my most authentic and best self. When I stayed true to my core desires, took action, and danced with the drama that crept its way in, magic seamlessly followed. My time in Thailand, Australia, and Bali served as my catalyst for change – to the life I'd always hoped for.

Pretty awesome stuff followed: I became a yoga teacher, met the man of my dreams, embarked on epic trips to central America and Europe, became an entrepreneur with my own events company planning fabulous, inventive, and inspired events, won a 40-Under-40

Award, wrote a book (yeah!), live a very nice life in Niagara's wine country, and I continue to proudly live the best version of myself. Whenever I applied the life lessons I showcase throughout my book, I tap into my creativity, my peace, and my joy.

And you can do this too.

Live your inspiration my friends.

Xo, Ang